D1146379

Don't worry he doesn't bite!

Tales of a Country Postman

LIAM MULVIN

Merlin Unwin Books

First published in Great Britain by Merlin Unwin Books Ltd, 2017

Merlin Unwin Books Ltd
Palmers House
7 Corve Street
Ludlow
Shropshire SY8 1DB

www.merlinunwin.co.uk

ISBN 978-1-910723-42-5

Typeset in 11 point Bembo by Merlin Unwin Books

Printed by TJ International Ltd, Padstow, Cornwall

To my wonderful daughters, Fiona and Lucy
and to my beloved wife
Linda
for her unfailing support and encouragement in getting
me to believe in myself and in my writing

Don't Worry, He Doesn't Bite

Above are the five simple words that have increased my anxiety levels over the years tenfold. Never a claim made by most dog owners, inevitably they are uttered by an innocent customer who truly believes what he or she is saying, namely that their dog:

a) Can do no wrong at all

b) Is as obedient and intelligent as Lassie

c) Can be controlled by said owner via voice alone

Only once in his career does a postman believe this claim – and that is the first time he hears it. Never again will those five little words bring him any other feelings except terror.

These words 'Don't worry, he doesn't bite,' are the opening salvo to which two further sentences will then be added.

Swiftly follows the most incredulous, shocked voice you will ever hear in your life, stating:

'Well, he's never done that before!'

Which then leads, as night follows day, to the third line which is delivered smoothly and glibly,

'You must have done something to upset him.'

When faced with any unknown dog, I wish to assure the world on behalf of all Posties everywhere: it is a dead cert that none of us has the least intention of upsetting anything that has teeth.

Most dogs are friendly whenever you meet them and that's in the nature of things. However, we do understand certain principles a dog must abide by. He is after all a pack animal by nature; and territorial and protective, he will defend his home and his pack if he feels there is danger.

The female can be even worse if she believes the young of the pack are being threatened; no sane Postie will get between a mother and her young: that's suicidal.

But in the cases of the 'biters', I look at the owners and ask myself: is it just possible the fault of the aggressive dog could lie with someone else, perhaps?

Royal Mail Shorts

One of the most frequent questions I'm asked as a postman is: 'Why are you wearing shorts?'

In fairness, this question is normally put to me in the depths of winter when it is raining, snowing, or blowing a hoolie.

Normally, before I have time to answer, I am thrown a few suggestions that the questioner thinks might be my reasons, namely:

Is it for a bet?

Is it for charity?

Has something happened to your normal trousers?

or – the most popular one –

Are you mad?

I don't recall ever being asked any of these questions as a young schoolboy back in the Fifties and Sixties when I wore exactly the same basic ensemble, as part of my school uniform. Nobody seemed in the least concerned about me getting cold in the depths of winter then.

The reality for me (and I expect a lot of other Posties as well) is very simple: wearing shorts is the most comfortable way of doing the job. We work a very physical day which is different from most other physical jobs in that we are constantly moving from A to B. From the moment I leave the office, I am walking; from the moment I leave my van, I am hurrying. I walk up hill and down dale, climb steps and walk paths; I am moving all the time.

Shorts keep my legs cool and stop me overheating; and most of us don't feel the cold when the blood is pumping through the old veins.

Of course, sometimes it's really cold. An east wind blowing snowflakes up the leg of your shorts is not a fun way of working, believe me. However, when it rains, I would sooner have bare legs than have cold, sopping wet trousers flapping around and clinging to me. Amazingly, bare legs stay warmer and they certainly do dry off quicker.

I learnt that as a schoolboy. Try it yourself – it works.

Surprise Visitor

There is a strict rule in Royal Mail that 'no unauthorised passengers' are allowed in the mail vans. I had one in mine the other day... and he came through the window!! The van was parked in somebody's driveway, I returned and climbed in, and there he was.

Sitting quietly in my mail tray on the front passenger seat, and looking like he owned the place, was a small Robin Redbreast. Did he know that postmen were called 'Robins' in earlier times because of their red jacketed uniforms?

Unafraid and seeming at ease in his surroundings, he watched me across the gear stick, and cocked his head on one side. I gazed spellbound at him for a moment and then grinned.

'I can't drive this thing with you sitting there.'

Unconcerned by this revelation he cocked his head on the other side before hopping around the edge of my post tray and getting closer to me. He then turned his head and his sharp eyes seemed to peer into every part of the van.

Obviously used to being in close proximity to humans, he happily hopped and fluttered around the van before flying up and standing on top of the steering wheel. He was barely an inch away from my hand.

Warm black eyes stared brightly at me from above a smart red breast, as each of us quietly regarded the other.

It was a magical moment.

'Nice to meet you,' I whispered, as his head bobbed up and down, before he tilted it first one way and then the other. Time stood still for a brief moment as he bade a silent goodbye, and then, with a flutter, he turned and flew out of the window.

That close connection, wild creature and human being, touched my very soul.

Bath Night

As I walk my rounds, I have time to remember my childhood and the different kind of rural life we led. Bath night in our cottage was Saturday night. That was mainly because we had church early on Sunday morning.

With a good fire lit in the copper and several buckets of water getting hot, we knew that that was Dad's cue to bring in the bath. Six feet long, it hung on a nail on the back wall.

Dad lugged it in and put it down in the living room just in front of the fireplace. The fire would be burning with a deep red glow. Mum would then switch the telly off because she didn't want electrics working with all that water about.

She and Dad would then fill the bath with several buckets of cold water before pouring in the hot from the copper. Then my little sister and I would be hustled into the kitchen and Dad would have first dibs at the bath.

There would be much to-ing and fro-ing to get the water temperature just right and Dad would settle in. He never got a chance for a soak because Mum saw to that. Within ten minutes or so she would have Dad out of the bath. He was expected to be washed and clean.

She would empty away a couple of buckets of water from the bath and then top it up with more hot before she got in. Ten minutes later history would repeat itself...then it was our turn.

There was me at one end, sister at the other; and Mum and Dad washing the pair of us as if our lives depended on it. The already grimy water went darker as our hair was washed and bodies scrubbed.

Then we would be dried off and into the pyjamas while Dad emptied the bath onto his vegetable patch.

What a performance for a weekly bath!

Circus in Town

You can see some very strange sights in our British countryside.

Forty years ago, as a very young and junior postman, I was cycling towards one of my more unusual calls. The circus was in town and my duty crossed the meadow where the whole thing was pitched.

I had been told to look for the 'booking office' caravan because that had a letterbox.

Turning off the lane to cross the footbridge, I glanced down the river and slammed my brakes on in surprise. A trumpeting cry greeted me as three elephants and their attendants waded out into the water.

With evident delight the three elephants proceeded to splash water everywhere as they waded about and submitted to the good scrub-down they were receiving from three stiff yard brooms.

Their huge size seemed very intimidating to me, and I was amazed at just how casually the three attendants moved amongst them. However, even to my untrained eye, I noticed that the keepers kept tactile contact with their charges, a simple way of communicating position and intent.

The elephants too, seemed to consider their keepers' positions before moving through the water. Aside from the vigorous scrub-downs, the whole thing was conducted with a gentleness I didn't expect. More than once, a scratch or a pat from a human hand was rewarded with an affectionate trunk lightly placed across a shoulder.

My biggest surprise however was the reaction of our native animals. The aquatic birdlife, after the initial panic, soon settled down and ignored the events taking place. Bobbing about on the disturbed water, they continued to forage for food, both in the river and on the bank, totally unafraid.

It was a study in harmony from three very different species, and a pleasure to observe.

Derelict Farm Buildings

There always seems to be the odd building or two in the rural areas I drive the post van which seem to have outlived their usefulness. They sit quietly, as nature takes them over.

Weeds start to grow up inside the building. Some grow so tall you can see their heads nodding out of the windows. Stinging nettles form huge clumps of anguish in the doorways which quickly prevent anybody going in to clear up.

Before long, animals and birds are the only life that enters the place. They drop seeds via one means or another, which in turn bring more vegetation into the building. It isn't long before some sapling grows tall and spindly as it looks for the sunshine.

I guess it is these saplings that end up breaking any remaining windows. Slowly over time, the wooden bits of the building begin to rot and decay. Insects, as well as the weather, will all take their toll on untreated wood.

It is now, as the building starts to weaken, that wind, sunlight and rain launch their most ferocious attacks on the structure. The roof is normally one of the first constructs to go. The wind lifts tiles and whatever lies beneath. The rain then enters through these gaps and does its worst, by soaking everything and destroying it. With sunlight warping and cracking what it can, it is not long before something has to give.

An old empty barn I drive by has been much ravaged by time and weather over the last year or two. Providing shelter for both flora and fauna, it has slowly buckled and creaked its way into oblivion.

The other day proved to be too much for it. A combination of driving wind and rain has finally caused this old building to partially collapse.

Its days are numbered now.

Broken Eggs

When I was very young, we lived in a cottage, on a farm on the Surrey/Hampshire border. It was an idyllic childhood and I was very lucky. One of only three children in the whole area, we were all given a lot of leeway by the adults around us. My mother told me of one such chap who lived to regret his indulgence towards us.

We three children weren't related and all aged about four years old. One early morning found the three of us, with our Mums, walking past a small farm and heading towards the village shops.

The old farmer had been collecting eggs which seemed to be hidden all over the place. He was carrying a galvanised bucket which he was filling with any he found. He stopped to chat to our Mums, but without consulting them first, he turned to the three of us and asked if we would like to collect any eggs we could find and put them in the bucket. He then compounded the error by turning the whole thing into a competition of who could collect the most eggs in the quickest time.

The Mums went white as we hurtled off around the farmyard and hunted for the eggs. Cries of 'Don't break any', and 'Be gentle with them', fell on deaf ears. Like the other two, I was determined to collect the most and be quickest.

Minutes later the three of us dashed back to the bucket with a handful of eggs each. To be first, we all had the same idea at the same time, and hurled our eggs into the bucket.

The noise resembled a 'splashing crunch' my Mum said. Three very embarrassed parents dragged us away from a very purple-faced farmer.

He never asked us again.

Christmas Eve

When I was very young, a great favourite on the radio was *Listen with Mother*.

A few days before Christmas one year, the lady from *Listen with Mother* told us a story about the animals on the farms. She said that if you were in the stables or barns at midnight on Christmas Eve, you would hear the animals talk to each other.

Excitedly, I rushed to tell my parents. My news didn't seem to fill them with the same sense of wonder that it had me and I was surprised. It appealed to them even less when I asked if we could go out to the barns on Christmas Eve and hear the animals chatting away. This incredible way of spending Christmas Eve didn't seem to interest them at all.

My parents and their neighbours all informed me that if I was outside at midnight to hear the animals then Father Christmas would not be able to visit the house and leave me any gifts.

But by Christmas Eve I had a plan... and it was a good one.

I lay in bed until Mum and Dad finished saying goodnight and my sister was asleep, before getting up and putting on my dressing gown. I slipped down to the scullery and got my wellies on, and then sat with the dog in the dog basket in order to wait until midnight. I figured the dog and I would nip out at midnight and I would hear the animals and probably see Father Christmas as well. Foolproof.

I woke up in bed the following morning. Not only did I not know how I got there, I never saw Santa or heard the animals talking. I could only assume magic had been used.

To this day, I'm still waiting to hear the animals talking.

First Wages

The first wages I ever earned were for standing with my little sister and cousin at the entrance to the cowyard in the village of Wishanger and stopping the cows from going in.

The men were taking the cows along the road to another field. The old chap in charge asked us if we would stand at the cowyard entrance and shoo the cows away.

For this first job I earned a threepenny bit; we all did. I remember rushing home to show Mum…and that was the last I saw of my thruppence.

The next money earned was when I reached eight years old. I started working with my Dad on his milk round; just weekends and holidays. Up at 4am with him and we worked a good eight hour shift together. Lots of dashing around and no chance of sitting watching him work. It was full bottles going in, empty bottles coming out; I helped him when I could for six years. My old Dad paid me the princely sum of a shilling a day for it.

Aged 14 or 15 I got a job as a paperboy. Seven days a week, I did three hours a day before school, marking up paper rounds and delivering a round of my own. I got nearly four shillings an hour with five shillings an hour on the Sunday. Some weeks I took home a fiver in total!

After that I went gardening and odd jobbing for five shillings an hour before finally joining Royal Mail on the princely sum of £14.32 a week plus overtime.

I've never earned a fortune but those jobs and responsibilities I had as a child and young man taught me that you have to earn your wages and nothing is just given to you. It was a very good grounding.

Climbing Trees

A couple of years ago, some old friends and I arranged to visit the area where we grew up together. We had all lived in houses that backed onto a recreation ground.

The huge gated field was in use throughout the summer as a cricket ground. In one corner of the ground stood the cricket pavilion and nets; the pavilion was a great place to play in if it was raining.

What interested us most of all was the fact that the whole field was surrounded by trees. Although some of the trees were fir, the vast majority were good-sized oak, beech, conker trees, and sweet chestnut trees.

For the next six years these trees became our world. Most had low branches to help us get up into the tree.

I spent most of the day up in the trees with my mates. We would climb as high as we could until the tree was too thin to hold us. None of us considered it dangerous to swing on a branch thirty or forty feet off the ground.

When the wind blew strongly we would cling to the trunk as it swayed back and forth and just laugh with the sheer joy of being alive. We would hide in amongst the leaves and watch the people walking on the ground. They never looked up. It was our world and we loved it. Sometimes one of us fell out of a tree; the branches broke the fall…and we always re-climbed the tree.

There is an old saying about never going back…you won't like what you see. We went back to our field, our trees. Every tree had been trimmed of branches to prevent people climbing them. Our world in the trees will never exist for the next generation of youngsters.

Country Sayings

My old great-granny had a large arsenal of wise old country sayings which she would fire off at a moment's notice if the need arose.

If the sky was red at night, she knew it would be a nice day when she got up the next morning.

On any morning if it was pouring down with rain, she would simply do her indoor tasks first, knowing that if it was 'rain before seven, it's sun by eleven'. She was certain it would be drier outside later in the day.

On the other hand, if all the cows were lying down in the field, she would bustle about outside getting her chores done before the promised deluge came down, indicated by the cow's behaviour.

One of her most favourite seasonal sayings was, 'Never cast your clout 'til May is out'. I used to puzzle over that one, wondering what a clout really was beyond the one I often received on my ear.

She explained that your clout meant your winter clothing and the idea was to always wear it until the start of the summer which she insisted started on 1st June. It seems my great-granny always wore a thick coat and hat from 1st October until 1st June, no matter what the weather was, because those were the rules.

I should think great-granny would have been furious to see me rushing around in my postman's shorts in the winter months.

She swore by these sayings and believed every one of them.

She had a point though. In that summery weather, one Saturday my wife and I saw two swallows swooping over the garden. The next day we awoke to a hard frost and barely any sign of summer at all.

One swallow doesn't make...

Dinosaur Machinery

Have you ever noticed how huge and terrifying some farm machinery looks?

The other day I came face to face with one of these, and in mere moments, I felt like I was its prey.

The small country lanes I work in are very narrow and twisted. At times I can barely see a van-length ahead of me so my driving is slow and painstaking. I approached a sharp, left hand bend at a slow speed. Cautiously I crept around it before slamming my brakes on in a panic.

Creeping the other way and now almost directly above my windscreen appeared the sharp-toothed bucket of some type of farm machine. It was attached to the body of the vehicle by an incredibly long hydraulic arm, which thrust itself up and out straight ahead.

If the bucket had turned to look down at me I would not have been surprised. For all the world it looked as if a tyrannosaurus rex had been resurrected from extinction and plonked into a Cornish lane.

Instinct took over and in a blink of an eye I had stopped, slapped the van into reverse, and shot backwards about twenty feet into a wider section of road. The analogy of prey and hunter loomed large in my imagination as the head on the long powerful neck turned towards me and advanced closer.

It was roaring loudly now and I felt powerless beneath its gaze. I knew I was going to be eaten! It crept inexorably onwards towards me before straightening up and continuing past.

The driver gave me a toot and a wave of thanks for letting him go by, and I was free to go.

An ordinary and normal daily incident had, for just a moment, given me an insight into hunter and prey – prehistoric style.

Drinking Tea

I switched off the kettle and tipped the boiling water into my mug. The teabag rose with the level of the liquid and settled quietly in the resulting brew as I added milk and sugar. In moments I had drifted out into the garden and perched on the wall to begin the process of waking up.

I looked into my mug and watched the teabag drifting around as I sipped my tea. I don't think my old Nan would have been pleased with my cavalier attitude which would have shocked her.

She never used a tea bag in her life.

Any teabags misguidedly brought into her home were quietly snipped open and the dust enclosed added to a caddy of loose leaf tea.

As her kettle boiled she would lay the tray. Doily first, followed by teacup/mug and saucer. The now-boiling kettle would have part of its contents swilled around the teapot. Once warmed; the water would be tipped out and the spoons of tea added; one spoon per person and one for the pot, followed by the boiling water.

The lid and teacosy would then be added. On a special ledge in front of the fire, an old enamel kettle would stand, quietly venting steam out of its spout.

The milk would go in each cup first, followed by the tea. Nan always used a tea strainer to catch the leaves as they rushed out of the spout. These were soon tapped back into the pot.

Sugar was added and the tea could then be sipped and drunk. It took longer to prepare than it did to drink. If the teapot needed refilling Nan would use the brown enamel kettle to top up.

I have to admit that my tea making might be quicker – but it never tastes as good as Nan's.

Fir Cones

My great-granny lived in a small Devon village all her life. Her time spanned the late Victorian years through to the first man walking on the moon. She witnessed a great deal of the progress of mankind and all the marvels and menaces of the modern age.

She also had a great way about her of ignoring most of these new things and sticking with the tried and trusted methods of her generation. Never a 'Luddite' nor closed minded to labour-saving devices and conveniences, she still preferred what she was comfortable with.

This was never more so than with her conviction of the benefits of open fires in the house.

'If I just flicked a switch to make the cottage warm and cosy I'd never get dressed in the morning. As it is I have to go in and out for logs and coal. I'm not doing that in my nightie.'

Her other reason for her open fire was less practical but just as endearing.

'If I had no fire in the grate it would be as if I had lost a faithful companion; a friend. It keeps me company with its cheerful glow and the way it flickers and crackles as it burns.'

Certainly, my memories of her cottage have always been of warmth, cheer and security.

She was always a bit ahead of the other local people when she would go up to the woods to collect fir cones to burn in the grate; always the bigger the better. From the age of sixty she would always say, 'I'd better collect extra this year in case I'm not here next year.'

I firmly believe that the fire and the jobs attendant to it, kept her going. I was only a little boy when she used to tell me that, and she was over ninety then.

Frog Underfoot

As a young boy, I grew up on the Surrey/ Hampshire border. In a very rural setting, our cottage, and the farm it was on, became the very centre of my universe. We even had our own little seaside in the guise of the Frensham Ponds, and this was only a mile from us.

In the Fifties, the water and the sandy beaches made it a wonderful playground for those of us far from the coast. We made full use of it.

One particular occasion when my father had a day off from his milk round, we spent the day on the beach. Dad's old van was stuffed with deckchairs, picnic, beach balls, buckets and spades and all the usual paraphernalia so vital for a trip to sea and sand.

Excited to the point of passing out, I jumped out of the van, sandals forgotten, and ran barefoot down along the sand to the water's edge. With no thought at all I sped towards the water so that I could wade in.

It was then I stepped on something soft and squidgy.

I glanced down before yelling in alarm and leaping back up in the air. Dad described my movements as 'doing a hornpipe' as I leapt about. My foot had landed firmly on a frog... and squashed it down into the sand.

Tears poured down my face as I looked at the poor frog pressed so deeply into the sand. They stopped though when I saw the frog slowly heave itself up out of the impression it had made and glare balefully around.

We looked at each other for a moment before it slowly hopped off towards a pond in the dunes. Still looking cross, he dived in.

I was afraid to join him in the water for the rest of the day.

Great-Granny's Manure

My great-granny Hill lived most of the first half of the 20th century in her rose- covered home, Porch Cottage, East Budleigh; at least it was called that until the porch fell off the cottage in a storm. I think it was the weight of the roses that did it.

Her back garden was a delight to the eye with strong flowers and delicious vegetables on full display, but the front garden featured on colour postcards for many years.

As a small boy, I asked her once how her garden grew so lovely and she pointed to a zinc bath, buried up to the lip, in a corner of the garden. To me it seemed full of dirty brown water and smelt funny. I couldn't see how that could help the plants.

However, as those sunny days of childhood drifted along I learnt a little more.

In a time of horses on the streets, and of small herds of cows and sheep being driven along the road, my great-granny had a use for anything they left behind them.

She would grab bucket and shovel and dash into the road before any of her neighbours had moved, and quickly collect what she diplomatically called 'their business'.

Rushing back into her garden she would tip the bucket contents into the bath of water and stir the whole thing vigorously with an old broom handle. Later the contents of the bath would be scooped out in an old watering can and poured around the flowers and vegetables.

I still couldn't quite understand the mechanics of it all then – but I knew it worked, and I knew it worked well.

Totally organic and totally free, my great granny would be mystified today seeing folk paying for the stuff; but that's 'their business'.

NCI and Animals

I wear two uniforms in my life. One is my postman's uniform; the other is the infinitely smarter NCI [National Coastwatch Institute] uniform. One is worn to deliver the mail, the other is worn for my duties for Coastwatch: I am proud to wear both.

My job with Coastwatch revolves mainly around the safety of the sea users in the area of our lookout. Land or sea makes no difference; we look after our coast and the people who use it.

It does surprise some people to realise we also keep an eye out for both domestic and wild life.

A dog running alone may have escaped its owners, it may be abandoned, it may be vicious, it may be afraid. Whatever it is, it can cause problems; and we monitor it in case it causes somebody some grief.

We monitor domestic livestock in case an animal falls over the cliff edge; or in case one wanders into a public place. No farmer wants to lose an expensive beast he has nurtured, any more than he wants his livestock to cause problems and damage to others.

Not far from our lookout a while ago, two cows stumbled over the edge. Unharmed but trapped, we spotted the problem and called the coastguard. Several hours later and with the intervention of a cliff rescue team, a vet, a lifeboat, and a helicopter, the cows were back in the field as if nothing had happened.

We also keep a watch for sea life. From huge basking sharks to tiny jellyfish; from seagulls to choughs; even whales, turtles and seals; we watch and care for them all.

Young or old, living or dead, domestic or wild, from the sea or from the land, fur, feather, or scales; all are watched out for and all are monitored.

I wouldn't have it any other way.

Jumping Cow Pats

As a small child, wearing a pair of bright new sandals, I once stepped into a cow pat. As the warm feeling rolled around my sockless foot I glanced down at the mess that was quickly swallowing the end of my leg and yelled out loud as I jumped back.

Mum was not best pleased and put me straight about the error of my ways with a well-aimed slap to my rear end. This was followed by making me put my foot under a pump as she sprayed freezing cold water over both foot and sandal in an effort to clean me up.

Finally I was clean to her satisfaction although a certain smell did linger. She was still telling me off when we got to my Nan's house.

This is where grandparents prove just how good they can be for grandchildren.

Mum told her the whole tale about my stupidity as Nan put the kettle on; and then Nan smiled and spoke out.

'That reminds me of you, dear. You must have been about his age when you did something similar. I told you several times to be careful but you wouldn't listen. You kept jumping over the cow pats when we were out walking with your father. Eventually it happened, you slipped and sat straight down in one, and it was fresh. We had to clean you off in a stream and your Dad had to wash your knickers in it as well. You spent the rest of the day without any on as they were too wet to wear.'

As Mum's face grew red, my Nan spoke once more, 'Surely you must remember dear?'

I watched the discomfort on Mum's face and smiled inside; I knew I would always remember, even if Mum didn't. Thanks, Nan.

Make Do and Mend – Part One

I called in to one of my ladies the other day with her post. Her farmhouse kitchen table was covered in neat squares of crocheted wool as she attempted to turn these squares into a blanket.

The squares had been crocheted by somebody else and my lady was joining them all together. She was enjoying the whole task immensely, mainly because of the therapeutic nature of the job.

I had no idea that knitting could be therapeutic; nor did I know that a group of ladies in the village got together each week to knit and crochet things for different charities.

I do love the practical skills that people hand down from generation to generation. My lady was delighted that her granddaughter also enjoyed knitting and attempted to make clothes as well.

I could imagine them both sitting at the kitchen table; the one with so much skill and knowledge to hand on, and the other so willing to learn and experiment.

We ended up having quite a chat about the merits and benefits of 'make do and mend'. In this time of austerity that we seem to be stuck in, the whole idea of knitting, sewing, and clothes-making, could well make a comeback.

As I walked back to my van I thought about my mother. She came from a background of the 'thrifty Thirties'; the 'fighting Forties'; and the 'austerity Fifties'. At a very young age I can remember that everything I wore seemed to be handmade by my mother. Jumpers, socks, gloves, scarves, and balaclavas: mother was always knitting something.

The more I thought of it, the more the memories started to flood back. I could see her in my mind's eye...making do and mending.

Make Do and Mend – Part Two

My Mum recycled things long before it became popular to do so. Nothing was wasted in our farmhouse: everything had at least two jobs to do; make do and mend. These phrases were Mum's watchwords...and she swore by them.

Evenings used to be taken up with knitting. Mum did this on an industrial scale. Long before I was born she honed her skills in the fiery furnace of war.

Whole flocks of sheep were shorn to provide Mum with wool. As a teenager during the war she had taken it upon herself to supply the entire allied services with woollen items.

Divisions of soldiers marched, fleets sailed, and aircraft flew, with, mother convinced me, all the personnel wearing Mum's gloves, socks, scarves, vests, and balaclavas. Her needles clattered like a machine gun, as a steady stream of garments appeared beside her.

Balls of wool bounced and jostled across the sofa as Mum knitted for England. If she had ever sent a communiqué to High Command from her battleground known as 'the living room', it would have read 'Send More Wool'.

By war's end, the exhausted sheep of the allied world had gone off for a well-earned rest; shepherds and shearers sat quietly in their sheds and fields and wondered if life could now be taken a little easier. Meanwhile the army surplus stores were stockpiled with Mum's knitted clothing that had survived the conflict.

Like the great secrets of the war that are still kept to this day, no official mention has ever been released of Mum's contribution to the war effort.

We suspect it ranks with Bletchley and is covered by the Official Secrets Act.

Several years later Mum got married and moved to a cottage on a small farm. Her knitting needles came with her of course and on she knitted.

Make Do and Mend – Part Three

The evenings rushed by in our house when Mum decided to do some knitting. The unwary would soon find a long hank of wool draped over both their hands and Mum would sit there and roll a large ball out of it.

Woe betide you if you slowed up the ball rolling by allowing a stray thumb to catch on the wool.

On other evenings, a coat hanger would appear on the back of the door. On it would be a much-loved, but beyond repair, woolly jumper. In moments she would be unravelling that and another ball of wool would appear.

All credit to Mum, she wasted nothing. Within a couple of evenings Dad and I would be presented with thick wool socks for the gumboots; warm and snuggly jumpers for outdoors; even the odd hat or balaclava for cold and windy days.

Sitting in our living room with a warm fire crackling and burning in the hearth, our thoughts did not often turn to how cold it could get outside.

Mum however never lost sight of the need to keep her family warm. Even my little sister found herself in knitted jackets and booties in bright and feminine colours. She always seemed warm enough to me sitting in her pram, but Mum wanted to be sure.

If there were enough oddments of wool, Mum would knit what Dad always referred to as her utility jumpers. Sleeveless pullovers made up of oddments were the most colourful things I have ever worn. From just below the V neck to the waist, Mum could use up a dozen wools of different colours.

Dad swore he needed sunglasses to look at himself in the mirror he was so bright and colourful, but we were both always grateful for her work.

Make Do and Mend – Part Four

My Mum made a small cottage industry out of supplying knitted clothing for wartime service personnel, charities, friends, and family.

Whether booties for a newborn baby or a bed shawl for someone elderly, she knitted for all. She reigned supreme with the knitting needles.

Today it seems so much more convenient and simple to buy garments that you need.

For all that though, I don't think you can beat something that someone has made especially for you. To know that somebody thinks enough of you to make you warm, make you comfortable: they're giving a little part of themselves.

I hadn't thought about my Mum's knitting for a long time until I saw one of the ladies on my post-round carefully sewing together squares of crocheted wool. It is a joy to learn that there are still hundreds of people, of all ages, who enjoy hand-making clothes for themselves and others.

Today, my poor mother with her arthritis has long given up the level of knitting she used to do. She still takes a keen interest in the younger generation knitting and will always pass on any tips and advice if it's asked for.

Do people knit more in the countryside than in the towns? I don't know.

Is there a generation out there who wouldn't know one end of a needle from another? Again, I don't know.

I mentioned this to my wife Linda the other evening and observed that I rarely see people knitting like I used to.

'Well, what on earth do you think I'm doing?' she asked as she held up her needles with yet another garment for a charity.

I had to confess that I hadn't really noticed until she said it.

She shook her head quietly but with sympathetic affection before picking up the needles once more.

The Slow Worm and the Cat

I was walking down a garden path while on a delivery and watched as a cat leapt out of the hedge and pounced on a bit of old cable sticking out of the lawn. Teeth grasping, he pulled, but seemed to slide off the end of it, before opening his mouth to try again. It was then the cable thrashed about a bit and I realised it was a slow worm.

Instinctively I jumped forward and yelled at the cat, which immediately leaped a few feet away, before turning and crouching down. Its tail lashed angrily as it hissed at me.

I couldn't leave the slow worm so I grasped it gently, yet firmly, before pulling it out of the ground. I had no idea that they burrowed underground and it was quite hard to pull it free. It curled up in my hand and seemed to look at me.

The furious cat advanced a pace at a time at me and looked so intimidating I felt it prudent to get away from the thing, so I moved off.

Once out of the gate I walked across the road but, glancing back, I saw the moggy watching me.

I am well aware that nature is 'red in tooth and claw', but I dislike the idea of a well-fed pet killing something just because it can.

It was a short while later in another road that I found a shady and slightly damp area of woodland in another large garden.

Confirming that the cat was nowhere to be seen and I hadn't been followed, I put the slow worm down on a sheltered bit of soil under the trees and left it to its own devices. Did I do the right thing? I don't know...but it did look very grateful.

Mum and her Stick Plant

My Mum Eileen has always had a way with house plants. She certainly keeps them alive and well for longer than most people manage. Is it because she talks to them, or gives them just the right amount of feed and water or because she loves them? We don't know, but we do know they thrive under her care.

Years ago, Dad came home from work with a plant that looked like an old stick shoved into the earth. He explained to Mum that he felt sorry for it, that all the others looked wonderful except this one, and would she like to help it? This was a side of Dad we rarely saw; compassion for a plant, indeed!

Mum took up the challenge. Firstly, she literally wrapped the entire stick in damp cotton wool. She spoke to it and told it she cared. Each day she would remove the cotton wool for a while, re-apply it later, and dribble more water along it. A month of this and a small leaf could be seen attempting to grow.

A year later it had grown into a fine rubber plant and was in its third pot. It stood in the far corner of the room, strong and magnificent, and Mum still fed, watered and wiped its leaves regularly, as well as talked to it. I swear if she walked into the room, the plant leaned over towards her.

One day when it had grown a little top heavy, a sharp gust caught it, and it fell, and snapped in two. Mum was upset but resolved to save what she could. I don't know how she did it; a cutting, or a root perhaps; but she still has a much smaller rubber plant today that she insists is a bit of the old one.

The Butcher's Knife

I put a handful of cutlery on the table the other day. All lay flat except for one knife which lay flat on its back with blade uppermost. It doesn't happen often but when it does I always think of my great-grandmother and the butcher's knife.

She told me that when she was a young woman she had gone shopping at the butchers. At the shop, she walked up to the butcher and asked him for sausages. He had been holding a knife and a sharpener when she came in and he placed them on the counter.

He started, 'Look at that, young Annie, the knife has laid down with the blade straight up and not flat. That's very rare.'

He nodded at her and tapped the side of his nose.

'You must make a promise that if ever you see a knife blade laying like that, you'll think of me. It's an old country whimsy.'

She promised him that she would. That was over 120 years ago. She told me this story in 1968 when she was already aged 94. I had laid cutlery on her tray and the knife had landed in that unusual fashion.

I don't know what the butcher looked like although I have an image of him in my mind. I do remember my lovely old great-granny though. How amazing that butcher was, to find a way to give himself immortality.

There is no way I will ever forget this stranger, thanks to that little country whimsy of his. My great-granny passed him on to me, I have passed him on to my children, and they will one day pass him on to their children.

I just thought it would be good to pass him on to you as well.

The Christmas Rabbit

Every Christmas my father would tell us the story of the Christmas Rabbit. In August 1948, he found himself a long way from home as he was living in digs to be closer to his work. His family lived a far more rural life than he found himself in – and he missed it.

The couple he lodged with, he always described as very nice people, although both of them had an excessive fondness for scrimping and saving. Dad always reckoned they both had the first shilling either of them had ever earned, firmly hidden in their pockets.

It was at breakfast that the man of the house gave my Dad his good news. He announced that he'd managed to persuade the butcher to get him a nice fat rabbit for Christmas dinner and he hoped my Dad wouldn't mind chipping in a third of the price for the said feast.

Dad's thoughts immediately turned towards Christmas at home. He had never known a Christmas when there wasn't a turkey and a goose for dinner. There was no way he was going to have a Christmas dinner of rabbit, no matter how fat it was.

He mumbled something about going home for Christmas and went off to work.

His boss at the building site, whose surname should have been Scrooge, was more than happy to give Dad ten days' holiday over the Christmas if Dad worked every Sunday for the next ten weeks for him.

It was a long hard ten weeks for Dad but he stuck it out. He always said it was the thought of the rabbit that helped him through.

He got home on Christmas Eve afternoon to the delight of his parents, brothers and sister, and he reckoned that year, the turkey and the goose never tasted better.

The Old Tin Bath

After years of using a tin bath we finally had a proper bath plumbed into the cottage. Although the war had been over for about fifteen years, Mum still lived by the Home Front 'Rules of War'. One of these insisted that no water in a bath should be more than five or six inches deep.

This was a major rule in our home and nobody ever broke it.

I digress…it's what became of the old tin bath that I wish to write about. With metal no longer required for spitfires or ships, Mum was now stuck with an unused tin bath… so she gave it to us to play with.

Dad's suggestion of making a garden pond out of it was dismissed because me or my little sister might drown in a pond.

The old bath became ours by elimination in the end.

In the summer months' Mum let us use it as a paddling pool. Dad's suggestion that we could just as easily drown in a paddling pool was also dismissed.

At other times, we would sit in the tin bath and let our imaginations run riot. First, it became a Red Indian canoe, then a sailing ship. It also acted as a car, an aeroplane, a space rocket, a train, a tank, and even a bed. That was the day my sister was found lying fast asleep in it.

One snowy winter's day, my poor Dad even tied a rope to the front handle, and exhausted himself by dragging us around the farmyard as if we were on a large Russian sleigh. I sat in the back firing an imaginary rifle at imaginary wolves to protect us all.

We had more use out of the bath as a toy than we ever had using it as a bath.

The Outside Loo

Journeys to the toilet in my granny's house could be fraught with problems, mainly because the toilet wasn't in her house – it was down the bottom of the garden.

What could be thought of as 'a bit of a lark' or a touch of 'how we used to live' in daylight hours, was a whole different game at night time. Walking along a sunlit path towards the little wooden hut beside the old hawthorn hedge and under the tree could be very nice on a lovely day. The plank with the circular hole cut in it was worn with use and pleasantly warm in summer. Sitting there looking around, you would see little bars of sunlight where the wooden frame had warped. A branch of the tree gently rubbed its leaves against the small curtained window; birds sang out merrily and you could hear the scratching sound of their clawed feet on the felt roof. It was a good place to hang about.

Not so in the dead of night, when the need to use the loo became unbearable.

Dressing gown on over the pyjamas, Wellington boots on the feet, toilet roll firmly under the arm, and torch in hand, you were ready to set off.

Bolt slid back as quietly as possible, followed by latch lifted, found you standing uncertainly outside in the dark garden. With only a pool of light from the old torch on the path, you would set out.

I would open the loo door and thrust the torch in for a good look around, before diving in and slamming the door.

Moonlight flickered and shook as shadows raced scarily against the wooden frame. The branch scratched eerily on the window; the sinister night bird calls echoed frighteningly close.

Strangely, I never hung around at night.

Staddlestones

As a youngster, I grew up surrounded by buildings standing on top of stone 'mushrooms'. The name normally used for these stone 'mushrooms' in my part of the country was 'staddlestones'. These buildings were normally a granary of some kind on a farm. Even some large gardens and parks would have buildings up on these stones to protect their seeds, bulbs and small plants.

Designed to confound rats and mice, they protected many seed and grain stores. The vermin would attempt to climb the stem of the 'mushroom', but were prevented from climbing any further by the overhang of the 'cap'. This stopped them from attacking the more vulnerable wooden building.

Looking like a giant letter T from a distance and a huge mushroom closer to, these staddlestones can be found all over the place today. Not always made of stone now, but often of concrete, they are rarely used for the purpose for which they were created.

Like many obsolete country items, these have become 'rural antiques' so that these staddlestones can be found now on my rounds as markers for a fence perhaps; or as a barrier to keep postmen off your lawn; or just as a garden feature.

I loved them as a child and used to think it would be so grand to sleep in a granary on top of these stones. I never did though. It is nice, however, to see them still in use today.

Solid and dependable, they are a constant reminder of a harder time, when you had to protect your family's food supplies from voracious pests. In these days of food bought weekly from a supermarket and placed in fridge, freezer or cupboard for days, it is hard to remember that some food supplies years ago had to be held for several months in your home, and if you lost them, you went hungry.

The Street Sweeper

I never knew his name but people said he was quiet and decent. I avoided his gaze.

He wore his old clothes with pride. The years had bent him almost in half. Solid army boots with hobnails sparking sometimes; baggy old corduroy trousers kept up with a length of string; an old jacket that hung further down at the front on top of a vest, shirt, and waistcoat; the whole topped off with a disreputable cap.

In front of him he pushed a wheelbarrow containing some carrier bags, a stiff bristled broom, a soft bristled broom, and a shovel. His whole future was in that barrow and he pushed it with dignity. Unspeaking, he coughed a lot. Permanently wedged onto his lower lip was a roll-up.

No matter the weather, he walked the local area and cleaned and swept every day. Then suddenly, he wasn't there. Rubbish stayed on the road and in the gutters, the streets looked unkempt and unloved. Someone muttered about pneumonia and mustard gas. Said he swore that the fags helped keep his chest clear.

Then he was back. He looked pale but still smiled a lot, smoked a lot, coughed a lot, and swept a lot.

It was then I looked into his eyes.

I stared deeply into the mirrors of his soul as he stared deeply into mine. I don't know what he saw in my eyes but I know what I saw in his. I saw a lifetime of pain, despair, anger, hurt, struggle, and loss. I also saw a lifetime of courage, defiance, pride, heroism, forgiveness, and dignity.

Nothing was said; yet everything was. I saw the life behind the man; I saw the man behind the barrow. He coughed once before moving on.

Fifty years later, I still remember him.

My Old Tortoise

As a little boy, I lived several years of my life on a small farm in Surrey. We had a huge three-sided barn which contained all the large bales of straw; nearby was a small granary. Although a wonderful place to play in, Mum was always worried about the rats.

We were never over-run with rats because the dozen or so cats living outside took care of most of them. These cats never came into the house and would avoid being petted or cuddled. Almost as wild as the rats, the farm cats' world only buttressed up against ours; the two worlds rarely crossed. However, the cats let me down once over my old tortoise; and so did Dad.

When it was the time for his hibernation, Dad would put the tortoise in a hay-filled box and place him in the shed. Here he slept through the cold winter and awoke in the spring. Looking back, I can only assume that Dad didn't even keep a check on the tortoise once during the winter.

That spring, Dad took my four-year-old self and my almost three-year-old sister to the shed to see if the tortoise was awake. We found the box on the floor and straw all over the place. Dad reached over and lifted up the straw – and all that was left of the tortoise was its shell.

I heard Dad mutter something about 'the rats must have got him', before I ran off crying to my Mum. For years afterwards my parents used to relate how my crying for the loss of the tortoise turned into screams of anguish minutes later when my little sister came around the corner with the tortoise shell on her head for a hat. I swear I'm scarred for life.

Three Deer

In the nature of my work I quite often have to drive in to the sorting office in the dark. It is a fine time to catch nature unawares as there is little in the way of human interference to scare wildlife off.

Not so long ago I headed into work on a morning of patchy mist. By chance the moon was full and beamed down from a cloudless sky.

I had already been struck by how beautiful the shadows of the trees looked as they stood out clear and starkly, cutting through the mist like scissors through paper.

Then I noticed a shadow move.

It caught my eye and I braked and stopped.

The shadow slowly lengthened in moonlight and became the sharp silhouette which emerged from the mist of a majestic deer. The elegant deer stalked forward from between the trees.

Behind him followed a harem of three females. They seemed equally majestic as their lord, but even their shadows seemed to be more delicate and feminine than his.

The four of them continued on their way, the dark elongated shadows they threw flickering in and out of the more solid tree shadows. Slowly they crossed the field to my left before stepping onto the road and crossing over in front of me.

As they got to the other side of the road, they and their shadows disappeared and I was alone once more.

Realising I had not breathed throughout the entire episode I let out a deep breath.

The whole episode is still one of my most beautiful memories.

Thick Broth

Mum could cook up a soup out of anything. A bit of bacon, an old chicken carcass or even a bag of bones from the butcher: any of these would start off the process.

She had a huge battered pot that would take a strong man to lift. This old pot would be placed on the range, and she would begin. The first things to be boiled defined the name of the soup for that week as they slowly turned the water into the all-important 'stock'.

If it was a bacon joint, then Mum would also place in some extras to boil with it such as lentils, broad beans, split peas, even pearl barley.

If it was a bony chicken carcass or a couple of beef bones, then Mum would boil those to death first before adding anything else. Mum would lift out what could not be eaten, and incredibly, would always find some scraps of meat to scrape off and throw back into the pot. The dog always got the sad remains of the beef bones while the chicken carcass was wrapped and burnt in the fireplace. She wasted nothing.

While all this had been going on, she would have been preparing all manner of vegetables and potatoes to go in with it. I can see her, stood in a cloud of steam, red-faced and clutching a wooden spoon of plank-like proportions. Sometimes used as a weapon of mass destruction on my person if the copper stick wasn't to hand, its main function was to stir the pot.

Adding anything that came to hand during the week she would eventually thicken the soup into a broth that almost had to be sliced out of the pot. It stuck to the ribs like no other food I have ever eaten and it did us good.

Wishanger Work and Play

We lived in one of the staff cottages on Wishanger farm when I was very little. It was a dairy farm owned by one of the partners of a large local independent dairy. My Dad was one of the milkmen, and that was how we got the place… that and the fact my Uncle Tom managed the dairy and was able to swing things for us.

It was idyllic living there; at least it was for a child. Poor Dad got up at 3.30am to get to work by 5am. Winter and summer alike, seven days a week sometimes; it was tough on him. In the winter Mum had to get up with him to help push-start his van: it was tough on her, too.

Mum worked a long day at home in a cottage with only one tap in the kitchen. The only heating was from coal fires which had to be looked after constantly. The clothes were washed in a copper and took all day to do. The drying was done with a mangle followed by a hopefully dry yet windy day. The cottage was cleaned with large amounts of elbow grease. It was hard work for Mum.

Dad did what he could to help Mum around the place, such as cutting logs, digging and planting the vegetable patch, and maintaining the old place; it was hard work for both of them.

For us kids however, we found ourselves in the greatest playground you could imagine. There were animals to play with, huge barns with bales of straw to build camps in and even sheds with equipment to sit on and play 'pretend' with.

On all sides were fields to run in, trees to climb, a river to paddle, even a country lane to play in.

It wasn't tough on us, it was idyllic living there.

Wishanger (1)

In the late 1950s we lived in a cottage on a farm. Perhaps cottage doesn't really do it justice: it was a manor house split into four cottages. Dad worked as a milkman for the dairy who owned the farm, and that was all it took to get our tied cottage. The rent was 17/6d a week and that was deducted from his average pay check each week of about £4. He worked an eight-day week followed by two days off.

We had little in the way of running water and what we got had to be boiled before you could use it. Hot water came from a kettle or saucepan; the boiling water for the clothes was heated up in an old copper; and a bath was a family occasion, one after the other, with heated water from any source being poured in the bath between occupants.

Mum cooked everything on an old electric cooker, but the house was heated by fires in every room.

We had a pantry just off the kitchen. You only had to walk in through the door to feel the temperature plunge. Thick slate shelves held all manner of foodstuffs. Milk stayed cold in bottles immersed in cold water jars; other dairy products and meats remained hidden and chilled behind great big muslin and net cloths which also kept out the flies.

On the other side of the kitchen was the room with the copper in it. Mum would light a fire in the grate of it and pour water in the copper. Once the water boiled and the walls ran with condensation, she would then devote the day to washing clothes.

When you think of the fridges, freezers, and washing machines we use today; oh, my poor old Mum.

Wishanger (2)

Our old cottage on the farm was a good two miles or more from the nearest village. Shopping was quite an expedition. Mum and our next-door neighbour (Auntie Shirley to me) used to get out the pushchairs and put the two small children (Susan and Brian) in one each. I, being about four years old, was expected to walk the four-mile round trip although I was allowed respite moments sitting in the front of Susan's pushchair.

The whole expedition, complete with shopping bags, purses, and shopping lists then headed off. Imagine Livingstone heading off into the African jungle: we looked a lot like that.

The long lane we had to walk up confirmed the old saying of 'the rolling English drunkard made the rolling English road'. Swerving and meandering, we slowly wended our way towards the small village that was civilisation to us.

Containing church, pub, butcher, baker, newsagent, post office, general store, and garage/filling station, the little village took care of all our needs including the spiritual.

The hour walking to the village, and the hour walking home, was also matched by the hour spent in slowly moving from shop to shop. Gossip took up as much time as the choosing and the buying.

Treats were few and far between although the occasional ice cream came my way. More often the treat was a drink of squash and a biscuit that had all been brought with us in a bag.

Bearing in mind we had left at about 8.30am, it could be gone midday when we returned back home. A cup of tea and a piece of cake revived the two ladies before getting on with the housework.

Mum now jumps in the car, does her entire week's shopping, and is home within the hour.

Wishanger (3)

Dealing with the fires in our old cottage was a thankless task for my poor old Mum. We used to have four fires permanently on the go during the winter months. Apart from the kitchen, we had two large rooms downstairs which we lived in the most. Each had a fireplace and a lit fire all day.

Mum would have to clean and sweep out both grates and re-lay and relight each fire almost as her first job of the day. She would also have to clean and sweep out the two fires upstairs in the two bedrooms. I used to love lying in bed at night with the warmth of the fire washing over me.

Tucked up and curled over facing the fire, I used to stare into its depths and look for castles amongst the coals. Shadows flickered around the room and up into the rafters of the roof above as I slowly drifted off to sleep.

The room took some heating as there was no ceiling above us. The room went straight up to the rafters and roof tiles. I have never seen ice on the inside of the windows as we used to have in those days. Mum and Dad both tried convincing us that a little chap called 'Jack Frost' had called during the night and had painted swirls and shapes in the frost across our panes.

Those bedroom fires were only lit in the evening and were banked up for the night as were the fires downstairs.

I can see Mum now with buckets of coal coming into the house; while buckets of ash were taken out and slung into the compost heap.

And now – all the heat she wants at the press of a button.

Wishanger (4)

We had a favourite breakfast at Wishanger that Mum would sometimes make us. She would get out the frying pan and slice off a lump of lard. The lard went into the pan, and the pan went on the cooker.

She used to then cut some slightly stale bread into inch-thick 'doorsteps'.

These would be slung into the now melted lard and allowed to cook. I can't remember how long she gave them in there, but she would turn the slices more than once until they were a dark brown colour.

She would then smear a generous amount of raw egg over one slice; and another, equally generous amount of crushed tomato over the other one.

Both slices would then be flipped over and allowed to sizzle for thirty seconds or so. She would then flip them back again, lift them out with a fork and let them drain, before sliding both slices onto a plate. Pepper and salt were vigorously shaken over the lot, and we would be slung outside to eat our breakfast.

The slices used to be so thick that as you nibbled into them you would find a white layer of bread in the middle that the hot fat hadn't touched.

Dad had the same but his slice came with a properly fried egg, a couple of sausages, and some slices of bacon. He wasn't slung outside to eat it either.

Susan and I would sit outside, sometimes beside the old well; sometimes on the old wall; or sometimes on the old seat under the apple tree.

I can imagine dieticians today going pale watching us eat a fat-laden breakfast like that…but it stuck to your ribs, kept you going all day, and tasted like food from the gods.

Unhealthy, probably. Fattening, possibly. Delicious, without question.

Travelling Dogs

I used to deliver to a stable many years ago on a round I did up in Surrey. I hadn't done that job for several months, and then covered it for one day. As usual, when I got to the stable yard, I changed over my delivery baskets.

I put the empty basket into the back of the van and carried the full one to the front. Sitting on my seat and wagging his tail was the stable's collie dog.

'Get out of the van,' I bawled at the dog and managed to shove him out onto the ground as I struggled to get the basket onto the passenger seat. I then went to close the rear door and found the other collie curled up in the original empty basket.

More amused than annoyed, I attempted to get this one out and ended up with both dogs now sitting in the back. It was the timely intervention of their owner that finally got them both out and my doors closed.

'The postmen don't swap baskets here any more,' he informed me, 'The dogs have taken to climbing into people's cars or vans and going off with them. Your mate should have told you.'

I admitted I hadn't been informed but would remember his advice. He patted both dogs and told me about the previous Christmas Eve.

'A nice chap came up from Devon and took away a pony in his horsebox. Five hours later he rang me and told me he had got the pony home – plus the two dogs as well. They'd climbed into the back. Guess where I spent Christmas Eve night?'

I looked at both dogs sitting beside my van and swear they laughed as he told me of the night drive he had to make to collect them.

Woodlark Calling

As children we taught ourselves the benefits of lying quietly on our backs in the grass and staring at the sky. It opens up a strangely satisfying perspective on the heavens, but from much lower down.

On most days we would look up through the waving grasses and watch the clouds. The object of this exercise was primarily to look for 'castles' in the clouds or other recognisable shapes.

There were other times when a large aeroplane would lumber across the sky. Propellers spinning and catching the sun, these giants of the sky would noisily go past with us boys checking excitedly if it was an airliner or a more interesting military plane.

It was fun.

Mostly though, it was birds that we saw as we lay there. Flocks of birds that not one of us knew the name of would fly over. Unlike the trusty airliner, these flocks were not as interesting as a group of small boys would like.

The birds of prey were our 'stars in the sky'.

Giving them all the collective name of hawks, we would watch in fascination as they either hovered ominously, or circled majestically, overhead.

To see one dive-bomb to the ground would become a talking point for weeks.

It was exciting.

And then came the day we saw a skylark. We heard it first.

I don't suppose we had ever heard a bird singing for the sheer joy of doing so. Several pairs of eyes peered into the heavens trying to find the source of that perfect liquid sound bubbling above us. We could hear it clearly yet it took ages to find it in the sky.

When we finally saw it, all we could think was how tiny it was to make such a lovely sound. We were spellbound. It was beautiful.

Ants Working Together

It is said that all grown-ups should try and look at the world occasionally through the eyes of a child. My grandson, Oscar, was busily looking at something in the garden the other day. I crouched down to see what had caught his attention, and still unable to see, lay down beside him and stared into the flower border.

A bumblebee seemed to have died and it was being carried off by a group of struggling ants. It would have been the same as a small team of us carrying away a dead elephant. As an exercise in cooperation and a show of strength, it was extraordinary. The way they worked together and for each other was amazing.

Two or three seemed to be guiding from the front and others behind kept moving up to take over from tired colleagues. No matter what was in front of them (and I confess I made it harder myself by placing a twig in their path – the equivalent of a six-foot wall) they overcame every obstacle and continued with their task.

Oscar was rapt with attention for some minutes before tiring of it and moving on to other things. I watched for a while longer, before realising I was lying sprawled on the lawn on my own. It seemed wisest to pick myself up and leave the ants to it.

I couldn't help but be impressed by this little group and what they were doing together. I guess the bee wasn't being carried away for a funeral, and assume they had a better use for it than that. I read once that in millions of years to come, termites, bees, and ants could take over the world. On the evidence before me that day, it may be sooner than people think.

Baby Robins

We have had some real excitement in our back garden just recently. Linda rushed down from upstairs the other day and dashed to the kitchen window.

'Come quick, Mully,' she called out in a loud whisper, 'Quick or you'll miss them.'

Expecting at the very least to find the garden packed with penguins or a couple of golden eagles drinking from the water feature, I rushed into the kitchen to see what was going on.

'Look over there,' Linda pointed delightedly, 'Look, Mully. Two baby robins have fledged and are in the garden.'

I could see two robins in the garden quite clearly. Red breasts looking a little battered and forlorn, they looked half asleep as they hopped across a tiny section of garden with grubs in their beaks.

They closed in on two tiny little brown birds that opened their beaks immediately to receive the proffered grubs. The snacks disappeared in seconds before the beaks opened for more.

'Why are two robins feeding two sparrows?' I asked in bewilderment.

'They're not…that's the two baby robins.'

'Where's their red breast then?'

'They're too young for that yet. Look, the parents are showing them how to feed.'

Linda watched enraptured at this little domestic scene taking place on the lawn. I have to agree it was a nice thing to see, but I couldn't bring forth the same enthusiasm as her.

In the end I found myself watching her more than I did the birds. Entranced, she almost had her nose pressed to the glass. It was like watching a small child outside a toy shop on Christmas Eve.

A short while later all four birds flew off into the camellia hedge and all was quiet.

'I've never seen that before,' she whispered, 'It was magical.'

The enchantment of the natural world: it gets us all.

The Trapped Goose

As a rural postman, I am well aware that a lot of isolated farms and cottages often have a dog or two running loose about the place. They are there to protect and guard. I also find that as I get to know them, in the main, they begin to accept me as a regular and harmless, frequent visitor.

I just wonder why this happy eventuality does not apply to the 'attack' geese of the rural world. Is each goose told, probably while still an egg, of the heroic defence that their ancestors performed in saving Rome?

Are they hatched on tales of small flocks kicking up a frightful din when danger threatens, which in turn alerts their humans of impending doom?

Whatever the cause, the geese of today are determined to live up to the past.

You can reason with a dog; not so with a goose. The head of the goose goes down; its neck extends with vicious beak ever closer to postal legs; a brutal hiss fills the air; and then it charges.

Eventually an old countryman tried to explain how I could get the upper hand.

'Make like a goose,' he advised. 'Put your head out forward, put your arms up in the air like giant wings, and then hiss and step forward. That old goose will back down for sure.'

Somehow I felt sure he was right, so the following day I put his plan into action.

Incredibly, it worked – except for one tiny mistake on my part. Never try to make a goose back down when it's trapped in the porch of the house. Its only means of escape was through my stupid body filling the porch entrance. You should see the bruises on my legs. Ouch!

Visiting Badgers

So often these days, the only badgers I ever see are those lying dead at the side of the road. There seems to be plenty of those. I know this is not a good time to be a badger right now and I have no wish to be drawn into a debate about the rights and wrongs of a badger cull.

Like most people, I don't know enough to give an informed opinion on the subject.

What I do know is what a splendid and magical sight it is, when badgers visit your garden in the moonlight.

The other evening, as we were falling asleep, we heard movement in the garden and got up to peer out of the window. Below us three badgers waddled around the lawn. They snuffled about, the moonlight clearly showing the markings on their faces.

As we watched, entranced, I did think it would have been better if they hadn't decided to dig a couple of holes in the grass. They then sniffed their way around the closed greenhouse and the empty guinea pig run, before heading towards the bird feeders.

They seemed to be merely inquisitive and just taking a look around. It was a moment or two later when they really blotted their collective copybook. This was when they launched themselves at the wife's spring border and started rooting up all the bulbs planted there.

This sudden declaration of war was met by the wife with a furious bang on the window and a snapping on of the light.

Three pairs of startled eyes looked up at us before, wisely in my view, they ran out and up the lane. It had been nice to have them in the garden. It was just a shame that, like certain visitors, they outstayed their welcome.

Bird Feeders

In the strong winds we've experienced recently, both our bird feeders blew down. Most of the ground area we use for the feeders is not deep and the poles can't go far into the ground. As a temporary measure, we turned to our old pear tree and hung everything up in there. It has paid dividends.

My wife gave the old tree a ferocious pruning last year which it desperately needed. Once she had finished we discovered that from our kitchen window the tree has taken on an unusual stance. Its main trunk is barely two feet tall before it branches out into six main branches. It looks like a giant glove cupped towards the house.

Smaller branches leading off the main ones have provided places to hang various feeders for seed, peanuts, fat balls, and half coconut shells filled with fat and seed.

It swarms with birdlife several times a day. Smaller birds such as chaffinches, tits, and sparrows, plus two robins, feed here regularly.

Beneath them at the base of the tree, the slightly larger blackbirds, thrushes, and occasional pigeons and pheasants, hop and strut about, feeding off whatever gets dropped, plus insects and worms.

It is an amazing little world of cooperation and tolerance on the birds' behalf as they feed happily together. The rare bird of prey does use our garden as a sort of 'fly-through' supermarket, but the tree provides more shelter for the victims than the metal feeders did.

Even our neighbour's cat has given up stalking in the garden, as he is spotted quickly and all the birds fly away until he goes.

Our temporary solution has now been declared permanent and the feeders have been consigned to lean uselessly behind the shed. Birds: delighted.

Forbidden Fruits

Years ago my granny found a crab apple tree growing near our local bypass. She kept an eye on it and as soon as the fruit was ready to be picked, off we would go. As a thirteen-year-old boy I would die of embarrassment as she shoved me up into the tree so that I could help with the picking.

Gran didn't care. To her this was nature's bounty, and there for anyone to collect. She had a good sense of where these fruits would be found as well. No wild fruit tree went unharvested if she had anything to do with it.

'Forbidden fruit is always the best fruit', she would confide to me with a wink. Gran kept half the family supplied with jams and jellies… and all from these hidden sources.

She finally got us both into trouble when she spotted a beautiful plum tree growing on a railway embankment. Coming from the generation so used to taking responsibility for their own actions, and not blaming everyone else, Gran saw no problem in walking out onto the slope for the plums.

That was where we both were when we saw the blue flashing light on the police car. We got off with a warning about trespass on railway property, and a lecture on the dangers of being so close to a railway line.

They were lovely plums though and looked and tasted divine. The two policemen must have thought so too because they went off with a paper bag of them.

Having been told off by the police, Gran would never let them down by taking the plums of the embankment again. The tree was cut down later that year and she blamed herself.

'Some fruit is more forbidden than others', she told me sadly.

Bird on My Hat

Last weekend I sat out in our garden and was engrossed in reading an e-book. The thing about an e-book is that there is very little movement from the reader. Turning the page by pressing a button barely registers. Even the wife is unsure sometimes if I am asleep or not.

The birds must have thought I was a feature of the garden because they were happily eating from the feeders in the pear tree, nearby.

Suddenly there was a fluttering of wings and a small bird landed on top of my hat.

Thankfully, I never moved a muscle and the little bird proceeded to hop quite happily around the crown of the hat.

I could just see the wife staring at me out of the kitchen window. She was smiling as she held one finger to her lips, as if to say, 'Stay quiet, don't move.'

The little bird – my wife said later it was a blue tit – continued to hop and move about on my hat with occasional little pecking movements into the material. At one point, it almost seemed to settle down on the brim as if ready to have a little doze in the sunshine.

Eventually a slight movement on my part sent him flying away and into the safety of the hedge.

I don't know what food he thought might have been on the hat or if he was just curious about this new platform in his garden.

It was a lovely moment and I like to think he felt unafraid of me as I sat there, although he was probably just blissfully unaware.

Whether it was trust from the blue tit or stupidity I shall never know, but I do hope it happens again.

The Rain

When I first came to Cornwall I remember seeing a phrase written on a tea towel. It was a phrase meant to amuse. It simply read 'It Don't Rain Vertical Here...It Rains Horizontal.'

Quite comical to read when walking around in shorts and T-shirt on a bright summer's day.

Recently we have all discovered the truth of that statement. I drove into St Mawes the other day and found myself in the very teeth of a 'sou'-westerly'. It was only possible to tell the difference between the sea breaking over the wall and the rain falling from the sky by the taste.

I fought the post van door open and attempted to rush into shelter. It was quite noticeable that the deluge of water that struck me was not coming downwards but was coming straight at me.

Later in the day the deluge continued and I climbed a flight of steps on the side of a house and discovered just what it must be like to be hit with a water cannon. The view from these steps is out over that lovely stretch of water, Carrick Roads, and is normally breathtaking. Any view that morning would have been nice.

Through half-closed eyes and clinging to the bannister, I ventured to climb. Stinging rain pelted my face and water found its way through every gap in my clothing. Nature let me know in painful circumstance just who was in charge.

My return journey downwards was even worse as the force of the wind and rain threatened to push me over. It was scary.

The following day it still rained, but this time there was no wind. Anybody seeing me would have wondered why I was smiling so cheerfully as the weather bucketed down.

It was just so nice to get back to normal... and experience 'vertical' rain once more.

Blue Tit Nesting Box

Great excitement from the wife this last few weeks as we have had a happy event in the garden. Last year in a moment of DIY madness, I got out the electric drill (guaranteed to bring horror to the wife), and proceeded to put up a bird box I had acquired.

It looks like a section of silver birch with a hole in it and a roof on top.

Neither bird box or wall seemed to suffer from my efforts, so signs of pending doom diminished from the other half. The bird box has sat idle ever since.

Imagine her delight a year on when she was able to tell me that a couple of blue tits were taking a great interest in the box. We watched them as they flew in and out with various bits of nesting material – and we waited impatiently.

I had forgotten all about it once again, when Linda spotted the male bird flying in through the nest box hole with a beak full of food. She has monitored the nest box ever since.

The little birds have been so busy at that nest box. One or the other constantly flying backwards and forwards with any food they can find. They are constantly near the feeders, or if not there, then grubbing about in or under the hedge.

Now suddenly all activity has ceased. No rapidly-flying birds shooting in and out of the box; just stillness.

Have the little birds not survived? Have they fledged and flown out into the world?

Linda assures me they have probably fledged and we should soon see young blue tits near our feeders. I cannot check inside the box though so we must wait.

I can't stand not knowing. Next year I'm going all-out and fitting internal spy cameras 'Spring watch'-style.

Butterflies, Bees and Bats

The wildlife in our garden is normally of the fur and feather variety. Wild birds of every size and shape or small scurrying mammals: all are leading busy lives in our small sanctuary.

Now we are being visited and settled by some other creatures. The old buddleia in a corner of the lawn has almost disappeared under the busy and fluttering wings of butterflies.

To my untutored eye there are only two types of butterfly. One is the humble 'cabbage white' variety; and the other is the more exotic 'red admiral' sort. Knowing so little about them, I tend to lump all butterflies into these two groups.

Looking like the butterfly equivalent of puritans and royalists, they dance in the air with exquisite grace as they head for the nectar in the large purple and white heads on the bush.

So too, the somnolent bees lazily buzz amongst these same flowers. Looking so leisurely as they float around, they disguise the fact that they are actually extremely busy collecting pollen. A small group of them have settled in a gap in the wall on the lawn. It's good to have them with us, and they are a delight.

These bees and butterflies seem to have declared a truce sharing the plants and it's a good example of peaceful co-existence.

With dusk coming ever earlier, we have noticed a new visitor to the garden. Flitting and flapping like a creature possessed, the bat swoops around the garden in the twilight as it hunts for insects.

We have found that by standing or sitting perfectly still in the garden, we can share the space with all these creatures and it makes for some magical moments.

Camellia Squirrel

A squirrel dashed across a driveway the other day. It was close enough to the front of the van that I instinctively slammed on the brakes. The van stopped as the squirrel launched itself onto the grassy bank before springing up against the trunk of a leaning tree.

It had moved so fast that I had not been able to see what was so odd about its head. In that split second of movement all I had seen of its face was a large bright red blob. Had it had an accident or had it been attacked by something hostile and a lot bigger?

I watched as it ran up the tree trunk. Adopting that move all squirrels seem to use of circling around the trunk, I was hard pressed to follow it with my eyes and have a good look. It took a sudden change of direction and its decision to run along a level branch towards another tree helped me. I could clearly see the squirrel now. Thankfully it had not suffered any harm or damage to its head and face area. It was holding a large flower head in its teeth and looked for all the world like a young girl with a floral decoration in her hair.

I don't know if flower petals are part of a squirrel's diet, but it was determined not to lose its prize as it continued into the next tree and vanished from view.

I mentioned it to the owner of the house who seemed as surprised about the squirrel's behaviour as I was. At least it solved the mystery of the missing flower heads off the camellia bush though. She told me she had guessed something was eating the flowers but couldn't work out what was doing it.

The Slipway

Since childhood I have wanted to work at the coast. The seaside was always my safe place, my bolt-hole, my refuge. After years of living up-country, my wife and I walked the South West Coast Path over eight weeks in the summer. We had such fun we vowed to move down here sooner rather than later.

It was meant to be, as my wife applied for, and got, a job in Truro and so we returned.

For me too, my dearest wish came true and I got a job as a postman delivering in Portscatho.

On my second day, I arrived in the early light and gazed out to sea; the waves rolled in beneath me on the beach; seagulls called overhead; and a red sky blushed down at me. Brilliant.

While alone, I decided to nip down the slipway to the toilets beyond. I then found out why it's called a slipway. I slipped most inelegantly and crashed down onto the concrete.

As regards injury, I was unharmed; but as regards discomfort; this was acute. I had slipped and fallen under the gushing spout of the storm drain and cold water was pouring over me.

I scrambled up quickly, and just as quickly slipped back into it again. Desperately I rolled over onto a dry bit and could stand up once more. Water dripped from me as I shivered in the January dawn and staggered towards the toilets.

Somehow I dried off as best I could before walking around the road back to the office.

Later as we worked, the post lady I work with said nothing about it save for one comment.

'Don't use the slipway as a short cut, will you? It's slippery and you may fall.'

Straight-faced, I said I wouldn't.

Compostable Waste

My wife Linda is always very busy in the garden or on her allotment. There always seems to be something to do and never enough time to do it. She loves it.

Her passionate aim is to be as organic as possible and this she achieves by composting as much waste as she can. Nothing escapes the composting bins unless she says so.

Needless to say, in our house there is very little in the way of waste food. As far as Linda is concerned, '2 for 1' is just an excuse to overeat or a ploy to get you to take more home so that you can throw it away instead of the supermarket.

The only food waste we have are peelings, used tea bags, eggshells and such like. This is mixed in with other, more interesting stuff that she composts such as tissues, torn up pieces of cardboard, shredded paper, even the contents of the vacuum cleaner.

This is all placed into a large bin out in the garden.

In another large bin is the used bedding from the guinea pig hutch. By the time it goes into the bin it is usually quite damp and often pungent. Seemingly it is highly prized by her in compost terms.

Alongside these bins, a small mountain of bags suddenly appears with waste from the garden. Dead-headed plants, dead leaves, clippings, grass cuttings; in fact, anything except weeds find their way into these bags.

The whole lot is then taken to the allotment where she mixes it all up in huge frames that I made from old pallets.

It always seems like magic to me as this unmentionable rubbish slowly rots down and turns itself into some very successful compost.

It's 'the circle of life' in action.

Crow's Nest

I have been watching a crow building a nest in a neighbour's chimney pot. There may well be a nesting pair involved in the building, but I have never seen the two together. As a result, to my untrained eye, I am assuming it is one crow working on his own. I imagine it as a male bird building a nest to attract a mate. I can only wish him luck as he doesn't quite seem to have the knack of doing it right.

His enthusiasm and work ethic cannot be faulted. It's the application that seems to be the problem. I couldn't begin to tell you how many large sticks he has dropped down that chimney but it is a prodigious amount.

Tirelessly flying back and forth, he has dropped stick after stick down into the pot. A friend tells me that the bird is hoping one of the sticks will wedge itself in the chimney, and then it can build the nest up from there.

If that is truly the case, then the unfortunate bird must be building a nest from the downstairs grate, upwards. Each stick must have dropped the length of the chimney because I am sure he has put the equivalent of an entire tree down the pot to no avail.

What has impressed me so much is the size of some of the sticks that he has carried. I'm not talking quite walking stick size, but he is carrying sticks that are as big as a riding crop.

The crow is a bird I have always considered a nuisance but now I am starting to admire them: this one is showing an industrious dedication that is rare in the world today.

Dappled Sunlight

Ever since I was a boy, I have loved sitting under a tree in direct sunlight. I can't pinpoint what is the attraction of dappled sunlight but I know that I love it.

Sitting under a shady umbrella on a bright, sunny day is absolutely fine and I do it when I can, but sitting in the shade of a tree with spots of sunlight trickling through is magic.

In our cottage garden we have an old pear tree growing strongly in one corner. Surrounded by the lawn, it also stands in as a permanent bird feeder. Its branches are festooned with feeders containing nuts and bird seed.

The birds congregate here en masse and consider the tree their own. Feeling safe from the young hawks that swoop down in open spaces, they think of the tree as a sanctuary.

I too, consider the old tree a sanctuary.

I slide my chair and table under the far side of the tree from the feeding birds and settle in.

Sunlight filters down through the leaves and branches and dapples the books and paperwork that I lay out beneath. It brings a magical quality to my reading or writing.

I am always happy to work under the old pear tree as sunlight dapples the work I am doing. However, the dancing light and shade takes on a meaning all of its own when I sit down on the sun lounger and fold my hands across my stomach.

This is the moment when I just sit in dappled sunlight and drift quietly off to sleep.

Dawn Chorus

I have developed a habit of waking up about five or ten minutes before the alarm goes off. Forty years of early mornings on the post rounds has probably accounted for that. I used to lie in the silence and watch the clock slowly move towards wake-up time. It would gradually speed up before I would press the alarm 'off' switch and roll out of bed.

Nowadays though, I am treated to the most wonderful sounds in the morning, and find myself listening with delight to the most cheerful tunes you could imagine.

I'm referring of course to the 'Dawn Chorus'.

Unlike Linda, who can identify any birdsong, my recognition is limited to a cuckoo. This doesn't stop me enjoying the dawn show, however. I can still enjoy an orchestra without trying to identify each instrument being played.

The notes trill and warble from all sides of the garden. One bird will sound the strongest for a moment and it is their song that leads the group. Then another bird, producing a different sound, takes over and puts his stamp upon the proceedings.

It flows around me a liquid. There is enchantment in the notes and there is comfort. I can only feel sympathy for those who sleep blithely on and are unaware of the magic outside.

No doubt there is a perfectly natural reason for the birds to sing so cheerily in the early mornings. But whatever the reason; whether it is an affirmation of territory or a warning; or simply for the joy of raising a voice; it is beautiful. At least now, when my mind decides to awaken me before the alarm, I can enjoy my minutes of wakefulness. It's a welcome start to a busy day.

Dumping Rubbish

Since I was a small child I have been brought up on the philosophy that if you have rubbish you must take it home with you. It meant you had to clean up behind you as well.

Like most country people, I take great pride in not ruining our landscape with rubbish. I don't dump stuff about the place and I despair of people who do.

As I go about delivering the mail, I have got used to the mindless characters that throw litter into the hedgerows and I have my own ways of dealing with that. What I can't comprehend are those who will tidy up their patch of countryside, but then dump what's been tidied away on somebody else's patch.

A chap I know has a small narrow drainage culvert outside his property. It takes away all the excess water off the hill and runs it down a gulley until it goes underground, through a pipe, and into a river.

This week he asked me to come along and help clear the culvert out. His concern was that the entire thing was now full of vegetation and he was worried that a heavy rainstorm could cause problems.

I agreed to help him and turned up this morning. To my dismay, his problem had been caused, not by nature, but by a neighbour.

They have a property above his and had done a beautiful job of tidying up a wall and border in their garden. It all looked pristine and gave a good show.

However, the waste cuttings from their garden had been casually dropped over the wall and into the culvert some twenty feet below. I appreciate the effort of making their own bit of the countryside lovely, but I feel they seem to have taken their eye off the rest of it.

Death of a Sparrowhawk

As a child, I was taught that even the death of a sparrow is noted in heaven. We lost our young sparrowhawk the other day and I hope it was noted by more than just us and our neighbours.

I also once read that if a bird of prey starts to use a 'bird-friendly' garden as a kind of 'fly-through fast food outlet', then you are doing something right.

We and our neighbours have bird feeding-stations all over the place. These bird feeders feed a large population of small birds. It is also a part of nature that small birds will in turn feed the bigger raptors.

We make it a point never to interfere when the hawks swoop down and fly away with a tiny body in their beaks or claws. All have a right to live and we wouldn't fight against that.

The young sparrowhawk though has become a bit of a favourite. He sits quietly in the camellia bush next door and keeps a close eye on their bird feeder. His other position is in our hedge where he can keep an equally beady eye on our feeders.

Beautiful plumage and a carefree spirit have made him stand out to us all. We are used to his zooming through the garden as he hunts. Sometimes he is successful, sometimes not.

Sadly, the other day he must have got confused or disoriented, because he flew into our neighbour's window. The impact was very solid and we all heard it. He swerved away after the impact and shot over the fence into the yard below.

That's where we found him, stone dead.

He was never the perfect guest because of his attitude towards our other guests, but we all miss him.

Different Paths

Linda and I enjoy walking very much and whether it's a short local walk or a national trail, we will walk for miles.

It must be said that the majority of paths, walkways and routes are very well maintained. The local landowner, who can vary from an individual, to a company, to a local council put a great deal of time and trouble into giving walkers access to these paths. Their contribution is vital.

In return, the majority of walkers treat the walks and the surrounding area with a huge amount of respect. Following the country code as a matter of course, they leave no sign of their passing except for the occasional footprint.

How sad therefore, that there is a minority on both sides that make life so difficult for the majority.

There is the tiny group of walkers who leave litter behind them like a trail of breadcrumbs. They will trample down crops, leave gates open, climb over dry stone walls, even take delight in frightening livestock. These are people with no regard for the rights of others and are a pest to us all.

Similarly, there are landowners who devise many schemes to keep people off their land. They deliberately allow the path to become overgrown, put up 'Private' signs, remove 'Right of Way' signs, damage and obscure stiles and allow the path to degrade.

We walked a path once that was flooded with water. The pipe under the path was blocked so we removed the blockage and allowed the water to drain down into the stream. A week later the pipe was blocked again, but this time more professionally blocked and harder to clear. It was no coincidence.

It's a lovely country and it's such a shame when a tiny minority try to ruin things.

Dusty Lawns

Our lawn is once more a bright green, verdant patch of grass. Situated between its flowerbeds and the path around the house, it is home to table, chairs, sun loungers, and guinea pigs.

The guinea pig run is moved around the lawn once a week and the little perishers look on the grass as a starving man would look upon a roast dinner. We move them just before the lawn's weekly mowing so there is always something fresh for them.

Back in the summer it all looked somewhat different. Whereas they normally chew their section down to the roots, while I mow the rest down almost to ground level; this year nature took care of that.

I can fill the composter with what I cut off in a week normally, but this year the sun came so much that the lawn resembles nothing more than the brown sun-burnt wastes of a desert. I could mow the entire lawn quicker than it took me to get the mower out of the shed. All that ended up in the grass-catcher was a few hardy stalks from some weeds and some dandelions. It beats me why nothing else grows except these things, but there you are.

The guinea pigs appeared to be putting on their own version of *The Grapes of Wrath* and seemed determined to head away from their dust bowl to greener pastures. I tried explaining to them that the grass would return but they just stared at me with concern and looked away to a greener field beyond.

Showing no interest in explanations of shallow soil and rock underneath, they fretted until the weather changed a while ago and the bit of rain once more brought the grass out. I live in hope they will remember what happened if we get the same weather next year.

Early Spring

The other day one of my 'customers' queried whether this was an early spring or a late autumn. She had a point.

Butterflies are still bobbing about on certain days, as were a couple of bees on the second weekend of the year. Considering it is still early, the temperature seems to be surprisingly warmer than expected.

It is in the gardens, however, where the world seems to have gone particularly topsy turvy; and my work puts me in many people's gardens. Lawns have not stopped growing, and even as I write, could do with a tidying trim.

Plants are still putting on a brave show and there is colour everywhere. At a time when the garden tends to look a little drab, these colours stand out more. Daffodils are glowing with a healthy yellow and look like patches of sunlight on the floor.

Cyclamen, an all-year-round plant, seem to be bursting out all over with their coats of many colours.

There are green shoots on all sorts of branches, and buds that seem to be straining to burst forth. There is light green growth on some plants, while brown dead leaves still cling to others.

Camellias seem to be coming out in full force and their colourful blooms stand out well against the glossy green leaves.

It is the roses that have amazed me most of all. I never expected to see roses growing throughout the year. This Christmas morning I was able to cut a stem and present it to Linda with her breakfast.

Not the most glorious or most perfect rose in the world but a rose none the less.

But for me, the most unusual thing of all is that I wrote this sitting out in the sunshine in our garden, and it is still only a Saturday in January.

Christmas Robin

I have always associated the robin with Christmas. As a child, when the cards used to come tumbling through the door, Mum would always use them to decorate the house. As many of the cards had a robin on the front, I just accepted it as a part of the season.

It was only years later that I discovered what the robin represented and to my astonishment, it was me: the postman.

I knew that the early Victorian postman always wore a red jacket. The idea was that this distinctive colour would make him stand out in a crowd.

He would also be spotted if he went into a Public House for refreshment; still an offence today if you are carrying mail.

But whatever the reason, the term for a postman at the time was a 'robin redbreast'.

In the 1800s it was customary for people to use calling cards. Cards were an efficient way to say a great deal without actually speaking to someone. It didn't take long for these to become very ornate, as people would often have them decorated to celebrate certain events. Having the words already written and with a nice picture meant that a simple signature was all the sender was required to do.

Christmas always has been the busiest celebration of its kind in the postman's world. The weeks of the Christmas card deliveries are our busiest.

With all the scenes that can be used on a Christmas card, it didn't take long before some cards depicted a smiling postman with a large sack, trudging through snow and delivering envelopes to happy customers.

The step from this scene to a robin with a card in its beak flying towards a house was an obvious one.

And so the Christmas robin was born.

Exceptionally Low Tide

It was only a few weeks ago that we had what the tide table referred to as a minus tide. Over a couple of days the tide was predicted to be exceptionally low.

Those in the know were saying that different bars and banks would be appearing in our rivers and estuaries which hadn't been seen for some time.

With this in mind, Linda and I headed down to a place called Turnaware, which is on the river Fal. We had been advised that a bar would appear that would mean we could walk out to one of the channel buoys on the river. Sure enough, when we got there, the bar had appeared. Joining several other people, we walked out onto what was normally riverbed.

The first thing we spotted were several large orange starfish, which had got stranded as the tide fell away. They lay haphazardly on the ground as if fallen from space.

The other thing we noticed were little jets of water squirting up at people: looking for all the world like the musical water fountain displays you see from time to time, this seemed to be nature's answer to a normally man-made attraction.

A chap told us that these jets of water being sprayed up were coming from clams. He told us that clams not only use this as a method of propulsion in the water, but also as a defensive measure to protect themselves. Certainly the clams only seemed to squirt water when people were close by.

We only had an hour or so walking around and kept a close eye out as the tide turned and the small pools of water noticeably grew larger.

It was a fascinating glimpse of another world which all too quickly disappeared as the incoming tide covered it once more.

The Family Allotment

The family allotment is now exploding with veg and potatoes for the table. I confess I do little up there as it is really the preserve of my wife, Linda. The garden and allotment are hers, and hers alone. My presence is only tolerated as a 'gofer'. Linda does the bulk of the work but I will happily 'gofer' this and 'gofer' that as required. In all weathers, she is to be found working happily away.

She digs and prepares everything before actually planting. This can be very hard work, involving a lot of back-breaking digging, bending, and general clearing of an area. Then comes the task, equally back-breaking, of manuring and feeding the cleared area. This and other heavy work she insists on doing herself and takes in her stride.

However, once that is done and the vegetables planted, she then fusses over her charges like a matron, and cares for everything as if they were her own children. Nothing is too much trouble as she sets to.

Almost overnight it seems that the allotment begins to respond to her and starts growing. This is then her cue to begin a meticulous weeding campaign. She puts in a huge effort on that, as well as the watering. At the same time, she launches herself straight into the never-ending war against the garden pests. How she wins in these battles I will never know, especially as this is all in her spare time – she puts in a full day's work each day as well.

Sometimes she looks so exhausted that you wonder if the effort is worth all the trouble. Yet although she may be tired, she perseveres; and then she comes home with a basket laden with fresh home-grown vegetables and some potatoes. The delighted and satisfied look on her face says it all.

Winter Snow

Even today I find snow enchanting. I know I have to drive in it and try to work in it. I am also very aware how quickly this country grinds to a halt when the first flake flutters to the floor.

I am even more aware how difficult it can make life for our farmers and fishermen as they struggle in bad conditions.

And yet the first snowfall of the year is always a delight.

That moment when you awake and notice a strange stillness and quiet. All sounds seem muffled from outside; even the daylight on the wall appears subtly different. You lie curled up under the bedcovers but there is a sense of excitement as you look and listen… and begin to wonder.

I always get up and reach towards the curtain, but only ever peep through a small gap to confirm it has snowed before dragging the curtains open and pressing my nose up against the window.

The sheer magic of the changed landscape takes my breath away. White folds of snow draped across lawns, flowerbeds, and the trees. Roofs wearing white caps of snow look as if they have aged overnight. My Dad liked snow in his garden as he said it was the only time his looked as good as everybody else's.

At this point it's time to get into the uniform and prepare for my post-round. You know your day will be especially challenging but fun as well. I loved the snow as a child; I still love it today.

Once out on the road and busy with the mail, it's magical. People are pleased to see you and want a chat; small children want a snowball fight or a bit of help with the snowman; some folk need a hand.

It's a different day.

Feeding the Birds

My wife is a bird watcher; she is also a gardener. Both are her passions and her delight. When we moved into our house the first things up in the garden, even before the greenhouse, were the bird feeders. We've had a garden full of birds all winter as a result.

Finches of every shape and colour congregate on the feeders and are more than equally matched by vast members of the tit families. As a man who can 'take it or leave it' as regards wild birds, nevertheless I have been fascinated by the activity through our kitchen window.

Hours can be wasted watching the antics of birds hanging upside down, feeding; birds hovering and swooping; even birds bathing in their own drinking water!

Sparrows, blackbirds, collared doves, and especially robins; they all set aside differences to come and feed.

Pheasants have discovered the garden too and regularly patrol the grass to pick up food dropped by the smaller birds.

One always appears, leading several females. Proudly aloof, he stalks the garden. He is like Mr Darcy amongst the Bennet girls; no doubt causing just as much scandalised interest as his aloof namesake.

Nature is 'red in tooth and claw' and there are the vandals, the thieves, and the wasters who loot and pillage our garden with impunity. The hooded crow (one of the Hoodies) destroys the feeders as it scatters food across the garden; the opportunistic seagulls (flying yobbos) attack the fat balls and break down the containers by sheer weight alone.

And the worst, my nemesis, the greedy, destructive grey squirrel (ASBO king) who eats eggs and even fledglings.

First Run in the Garden

The two guinea pigs have spent all winter living in our greenhouse. This has kept them safe, dry, and warm during the cold months just gone. Their hutch sits comfortably on the floor of the greenhouse and they have a huge area to run and play in. Liberal use of hay and an absorbing layer of newspapers has kept them happy, as have various chewy things and objects to keep them busy.

Linda supplies them with all the cuddles they need and has kept them clean and tidy with liberal use of brushes and claw clippers. Even I have been known to spoil them with the odd sprig of parsley now and again.

Last Sunday it looked for a short while as though winter was behind us. I had settled myself in the old garden chair with a book and Linda was pottering at her usual frenzied pace.

I looked up to see her reversing out of the greenhouse clutching the hutch, before she turned and placed it inside the old run that was still sitting on part of the lawn. She then opened the door of the hutch which doubles as a ramp and stepped quickly out of the run.

Two twitching noses appeared in the small doorway, followed by two open-mouthed furry faces. They gazed enraptured at the lush green lawn before launching themselves down the ramp.

Both faces dived into the grass; both jaws started chomping. Like two out-of-control lawnmowers, they zoomed back and forth across the grass.

I have never witnessed gluttony like it. An hour later, two bloated bodies were carefully put back into the greenhouse, where they lay digesting the lawn in the afternoon sun.

What a simple, yet happy life they both live.

Flying Geese

I love watching birds in flight. Whether it's a lone buzzard circling lazily and calling to the heavens; a seagull screaming at the world as it zooms across a beach looking for unwary humans; or a murmuration of twittering starlings as they perform the most wonderful and intricate aerial ballets against the sky... all are brilliant.

However, it is the humble goose that always calls me and brings me running to the door. I find them irresistible.

Their distinctive honking cry is always the first thing you notice about them. Distant at first, you can hear the sound getting louder as they get closer.

If they come close enough you can hear the strong beat of their wings as they push their way through the sky. It is a hint of places far away; of their secret places; it gives a sense of age-old travel.

And it is not only the sound that pulls at me. Their formation in flight is a geometric design of great beauty. That huge V against the sky, pointing to distant destinations as the birds fly onwards, is a reminder that my own feet are firmly on the ground and I'm going nowhere.

As I go to work I notice they have been gathering in our estuary for weeks now and the birds cover the water in every direction. Small groups take off and fly east before returning later in the evening. The noise is deafening, the activity frenzied; there is a sense of anticipation.

I know it won't be long before squadrons of the geese will take off and not be back until next year. They go, I stay.

I shall look forward to welcoming them back next year...but sometimes I wish I could go with them.

Llamedos

We postmen like houses with numbers. You can swiftly count your way along a street and locate the property you are after. A house name with no number, in a road where you are delivering parcels, however, results in you creeping along, head swivelling back and forth like radar, as you try to locate the place.

Beech Cottage can be self-explanatory if you spot a large beech tree in a garden. The Pink House is easily found if it is the only pink house in a road. Thatched Cottage speaks for itself.

It's when you get a name like Mon Repose, or Fred-Dora, or Capri Sunset; that's when you struggle. Some house names are nailed to a tree, which is fine in winter but useless in summer. Some are faded, some overgrown, some are even missing altogether.

Slowly the van creeps along the road, flashers flashing... then you spot the house and slam the brakes on. The bloke behind you, already annoyed about you creeping along, has now almost rammed the back of the van. He gets even crosser as you jump out of the van and launch yourself at the house in question. It really is amazing how quickly you forget about everything else when you are just focussed on getting rid of an item of post and are trying to find the property.

House names can tell you much though. Soldiers Rest, Dunworking; these can explain the people inside. The Old Chapel, The Old School House; these explain the building's original use. St Helena or Mumbles explains either a favourite holiday place or a previous home.

Some are inexplicable like Atlantic View. Not in St Mawes it's not...that's the Channel out there.

And as for Llamedos...No, it is not a Welsh word, nor old English. Even I know that backwards it says Sod 'em All.

Fur and Feather

There is now a new resident in our garden who seems to have moved in permanently. He is a small mouse who appears to have spent the winter living in our shed and quietly helping himself to the bird food. Small tooth marks in the fat balls and spilled bird seed on the floor were a bit of a giveaway.

A small hole in one corner of the floor confirmed his entrance. We have secured the bird food but, following the old adage that there is room in the garden for both fur and feather, we do leave the occasional crumbs on the shed floor for him.

Sometimes you can spot him from the kitchen window as he hurries along the very edge of the path. He protects himself by keeping close to the old Cornish dry stone wall that runs along its edge. What is a small wall, just one step up onto our lawn, must appear like a large escarpment to him.

He pauses in various places to peer around and ensure all is well, before moving on. His journey eventually gets him onto the lawn and under the old pear tree where our bird feeders are. Here he hunts about in the grass and picks up what fallen or scattered bird seed he can get before the birds take it.

He then retreats onto the path and heads for a gap in the stone wall which is a perfect mouse-sized cave. Here he can crouch in the sheltered sunshine and watch the world go by as he quietly digests his food. He is no bother at all and proves the old 'fur and feather' adage is, happily, not a myth.

Health and Safety

As a normal person who uses his own common sense to survive the perils of life, I confess to finding certain aspects of 'Health and Safety' a little annoying and ridiculous. I'm a firm believer in taking responsibility for my own actions and I loathe the compensation culture which allows someone to place the responsibility of their own actions with someone else.

A case in point was a recent visit to a garden centre. I wished to purchase two items. One item was a pair of secateurs; the other a small hand axe. The secateurs were hidden behind a glass door securely fastened with lock and chain. I summoned an assistant.

She unlocked the door and handed me the pair I wanted to look at, but only after re-locking the door. I couldn't get much of a look at the item because the bladed part was contained inside a strong tamper-proof plastic container. I could make them work but couldn't physically touch the blade.

The assistant explained to my perplexed enquiry that they are all like this now because of Health and Safety. Seemingly, 'they' wouldn't want me running riot in the garden centre with the secateurs, taking people hostage.

Finally agreeing to buy one pair, I asked her if I could also purchase a small hand axe.

'Certainly,' she said as she walked off. She pointed towards the wall where there was a long line of various axes with no 'guards', just waiting for anybody to pick one up: Help yourself.

For once, I was rendered speechless. Can the powers that be see the absurdity of this situation or is it just me being difficult?

Horse Flies

I think there is a good case for the notion that horse flies wear carpet slippers. My old Granddad insisted they wore them. Either that or they have learnt to levitate just above my skin without a beat of their wings. There is certainly a stealth about them that beggars belief.

But no matter what part of my body it is, and bear in mind I wear shorts as a postman so it's often the leg, the first I am aware of them being close by is when there is a sharp pain and they start to feed. The inevitable slap at the injured part of my body normally results in the demise of the hungry fly, and a minute smear of blood on my hand.

Invariably I end up with a red hand-print on myself which surrounds a painful and soon-to-be-raised lump of a bite. Then it all starts to throb and to itch.

My point is, though, that I never notice the horse fly until it bites. Any other insect that lands on me and starts to crawl about is normally felt instantly. Before any harm is done, a casual flap of the hand in its direction is enough to get it to leave you alone.

This is why I suspect the humble horse fly has evolved and learnt some amazing stealth technique in its bid for food. In that respect nature is continuously brilliant at what it does.

There seems no end to the constant evolving of creatures in their respective bids to reproduce, stay safe, and eat.

However, if ever I manage to catch one that I haven't squashed flat while protecting myself, I will hold it up in the air by the scruff of its neck and do my own research about the carpet slippers. Granddad just may have been right after all.

Can't you just reverse?!!

When I worked as a postman in Surrey/Hampshire, I got very used to working off the beaten track. I knew the width of my van and its length; I knew the lanes intimately; and I could reverse for miles by means of my wing mirrors. It was just as well really, because drivers cutting through from the dual carriageway to the motorway didn't have a clue.

Locals constantly bemoaned the speed of the vehicles taking a short cut: the enormous size of them; their insistence on hogging the middle of a single track lane; and the total inability of the drivers to reverse.

Several times a day, I would find myself reversing the post van 500 yards, because the car I was facing could not reverse the 10 yards back into a farm gateway. I would also reverse miles because the driver facing me usually needed at least two feet either side to negotiate the road.

'Can you pull over, please?'

'No I can't, Postie, she's a new car. Pull your old van into the hedge or can't you just reverse?'

Some days I went backwards more times than forwards.

Did this course of events change on moving to Cornwall? Not a bit of it!!

I appreciate that most holidaymakers are not used to our tiny lanes and that their vehicles are probably hugely expensive.

But it would be so helpful if the holidaymaker could just pull in a bit, or reverse.

Dave came back the other day shaking his head in disbelief.

'I just had to reverse nearly quarter of a mile. I met a lady in a big Chelsea tractor. I asked her to reverse into the lay-by so I could squeeze past. It was only 10 feet.'

Her answer, 'Sorry Postie, it's a new car and I can't help you there, because it's not fitted with reverse.'

Dave knew when he was beaten!!

Horses in a Field

An empty field near our old Surrey home once acquired four ponies. They appeared overnight and were found grazing in the morning by the owner. He also found the chain and padlock, which had been on the gate, lying in several pieces on the ground. An old piece of rope now held the gate shut.

The ponies were described as 'gypsy ponies', and all seemed in fairly good condition. He reported it at once, but was told he would have to speak to the owner of the ponies if they should turn up again. He was reluctant to do this however, and as he lived some distance from the field anyway, decided to leave a letter, in a plastic bag, on the gate.

The letter simply asked the owner to remove the ponies from off his land and to take them somewhere else. He pointed out that it was private property.

His letter was replied to a couple of days later in very basic and earthy tones and the ponies remained.

They remained for two days in fact before disappearing overnight. We assumed the owner had decided to do the right thing and remove them. This happy state of affairs was proved wrong when the owner of the ponies turned up in the village demanding to know where his livestock had gone.

Nobody could shed any light on the subject and the angry man was eventually moved on by our local village copper. It was years later that I found out the truth.

It seemed that a quiet phone call to a 'friend of a friend', resulted in all four ponies being spirited away to a pony trekking centre somewhere in the West Country where they lived a very happy and fulfilling life.

They called it 'old-fashioned justice'.

January Daffodils

I am amazed at the number of daffodils that have burst into flower in the first week of January. The first clump I spotted as I did my rounds were standing bravely in a sunny patch of grass on a bank. It was such a spring-like picture, as beautiful as it was unexpected.

Since then I have spotted quite a few more daffodils providing a welcome dash of colour against the darker greens and browns of winter.

They reminded me of my own daffodil bulb that I planted at home. Back in the spring of last year I was out at work, when I accidentally kicked something on the road.

I glanced down to see what it was and spotted a very sad looking bulb rolling across the tarmac. It was partly crushed as if a size ten boot (mine) had just trodden on it and also had a fairly deep cut about a third of the way through.

I picked the poor battered thing up and put it into the van door pocket. It spent the rest of the day being bounced around and rolling from side to side as I went about my work.

Then I brought it home.

The resigned expression on my wife's face said it all, as I showed her yet another abandoned 'waif and stray' I'd picked up on my rounds, which I felt should be given a second chance. I took one of her pots and a handful of her precious compost and planted the bulb. The whole thing I then placed in a quiet corner of the garden and left it alone.

Reminded of this I looked for it when I got home the other day. There is no glowing yellow flower as yet... but the bright green shoots of recovery as it grows quietly in its spot delighted me beyond measure.

Labrador Generations

I saw a wonderful sight as I delivered the mail a while ago; a man and his wife walking with five black labradors. It was like the canine version of the Seven Ages of Man.

Firstly there was a very young puppy waddling along. Inquisitive and excited, he examined and scampered his way along with moments of sitting down exhausted and calling to be carried by the lady. This she did.

The second was about two or three years old and was into everything as he lolloped about in a clumsy, adolescent way, tongue hanging out and crashing through everything in his path. The older dogs pinned him down more than once.

The next oldest, aged about six I would guess, was a dog of great strength and stamina, and had a great sense of being the 'heir apparent' in the pack. Loose-limbed and eager he was only a year or so from being leader of the pack. He still liked to run and play with the younger dogs.

In front of them all and looking every inch the boss was a magnificent dog. Very much in command and wearing his authority as if by divine right, he walked alone, yet close to the humans in his pack. His bark encouraged the pup, yet kept the other two dogs firmly in their place. He was about ten.

Walking alongside the man was an incredibly old dog. His arthritis was letting him down but he gamely walked on in his place beside his master. If he knew the dog leader just behind him was keeping a benevolent eye on him, he gave no sign.

Struggling and slow yet determined, his grizzled jaws drooping and dripping; he kept pace and looked at his master with adoring eyes.

All life was there in one pack of dogs.

Little Egrets

I must have been fifty years old when I saw my first egret. I can remember my wife spotting it as we were walking in the New Forest. She told me it was a little egret and we watched it for some time as it busied itself on the mud banks along the river.

It looked such an exotic creature with that beautiful white plumage, long legs and its dagger-like beak. All these things combined to make it seem as if it must have been blown here from some foreign country far away.

Then it flew off and disappeared behind the trees. It was such a privilege to see this elegant and delightful creature that must so obviously be rare.

I never thought I would see another one in the wild.

Then we moved down here to Cornwall and now live beside a tidal estuary.

Suddenly, my exotic and rare bird has become about as unusual as a robin in the back garden. They are all over the place.

There is nothing quite as enchanting as seeing a small group of egrets feeding together socially in the evening. They are generally quite quiet.

There are moments of insanity though, when, some of them rush around with wings flapping madly as they dash about. It becomes bedlam for a while.

Then there long spells when they just seem to quietly stand still and go about the business of feeding themselves.

It is so odd though, to think that for at least fifty years, I had never seen one at all. I still think of them as rare and exotic, even though all of a sudden, I seem to be up to my eyes in the things.

Magic and the Buzzard

I have a great respect and regard for all the raptors of our avian world. Their grace in flight and their skill in the hunt is incredible. There are buzzards near us which look so effortless as they glide serenely across the sky. Occasionally calling out, they swerve and dance in the air as they scan the ground.

Sparrowhawks hover nearby and hang almost motionless as they await something to eat.

The other day a large fat pigeon waddling around our garden suddenly vanished in an explosion of feathers and fury as a hawk crashed down on it. Mercifully the hawk hunched over its prey with its wings cupped around it, which spared us from watching its eating habits.

I was far more delighted though with the antics of a buzzard, and next-door's cat, Magic, the other day.

A young rat appeared under the bird feeders and began to hunt for bits of seed. Without warning, Magic leapt out of hiding and killed the rat with an incredible swiftness. He shook it a few times and patted it about before losing interest and moving on.

I did grumble about the cat as I put my boots on, prior to going out and removing the rat's body. I really thought he could have taken it with him!

Boots on, I stood up in the kitchen and watched in surprise as a buzzard flew down into the garden, grabbed the rat, and flew off with it. I'm sure Magic and the buzzard weren't working together, but as an example of cooperation and efficiency, it took some beating.

Moonlight

We are lucky in our village to have very little artificial light. Apart from the odd security glare that sometimes flashes into life, we only tend to see reflective glow from cottage windows.

This means that on cloudy, dark nights, you really need a torch to get around the place. It also means that on clear, dark nights the sky is full of stars; and it is beautiful.

I can always pick out the distinctive shapes of the Plough, Cassiopeia, and Orion. I can even find the Pole Star. These familiar and friendly constellations are in fact the only ones I can pick out with accuracy. They glitter above us and cast a comforting yet fragile light about the place.

My favourite nights though, are the cloudless nights on and around the full moon. A whole new world is illuminated, familiar yet different.

As a child, I would love to peep out of the bedroom window and look at the stark world of black and white that was displayed before me. It was the lack of colour, where normally there would be nothing but colour, that intrigued me.

My normal outlook on the world seemed simpler. The moonlight brought memories of the colourless world of our Fifties television set into life all around me. Areas of shades of shadow competed against areas of white light. It fascinated me then as it does today.

Over all of this, a benign full moon, face clearly seen, would beam down on my world. I had no idea then of her strength as she changed the tides and moved mountains of seawater.

I am older now; supposedly wiser; yet I love nothing more than gazing out of my window and seeing the moonlit night with the eyes of a child.

Moss on the Roof

How do clumps of moss form on the roof of my house? The wretched stuff just seems to appear there and sits haphazardly and untidily for all to see. I have been told it means that no heat is escaping through the roof, so that's a bonus I suppose.

I don't have a ladder long enough to reach the roof, and if I did, I probably wouldn't be too happy about climbing up there to clean the moss off.

I am unsure how moss even grows. It seems to bring everything it needs to my roof when it does turn up. Somehow it seems to supply its own earth as well. It's all very odd.

For some reason which escapes me, the local birdlife does seem to take great delight in clearing my roof for me. I can be sitting quite happily in the garden when I notice lumps of the green stuff dropping down around me.

Invariably, as I stand up to pick a lump of moss out of my shirt collar, I notice a bird or two up on the roof. Not always huge birds either. I look up expecting to see seagulls and sometimes it is just a sparrow or a starling.

My assumption, which is based on the odd bit of moss I have picked up and examined, is that the moss seems to harbour a lot of insects. I guess it is these that the birds are after when the moss falls away.

If the moss does provide a food source for the bird life around us, then of course I am not going to complain about it growing on my roof at all.

But it still doesn't explain to me how it gets up there in the first place.

Mother Nature's Great Plan

I attempted a good deed the other day. They say you should never interfere with nature's great plan but I made an exception.

In our garden shed I found a bumblebee hopelessly stuck in a spider's web. Buzzing furiously, it was attempting to free itself and getting more entangled as it did so. Deciding to deny the spider its meal I scooped my hand through the web and rescued the bee. There was no sign of a half-starved or angry spider, but I still beat a retreat to the safety of our kitchen.

The bee was still struggling in the sticky strands and now seemed to be glued to my palm. I grabbed a couple of cotton buds from a drawer, and as gently as possible, attempted to clean up the bee. As if aware of my efforts, the bee finally resigned itself to my ministrations, and even coped with the most undignified positions that I put her in. She sat still in my half-clenched fist as I got the worst off her.

Then she started to buzz in my hand and I held my arm aloft and let her fly up into the sky. I could only hope any residue would soon be dealt with by the bee herself.

Without a word of thanks or even a backward glance, she flew up into the wild blue, as I watched her go. As I watched her recede into a small dot, as a bird suddenly flew down and snapped her out of the very air. It was gone, and Mother Nature proved once more that she is very much in charge. She will accept some interference, both good and bad; but no matter how well-meaning our efforts are, she does prefer to stick to her own plan.

Night Noises

As a postman, I'm used to waking up very early but not usually in the night. Yet I woke up the other night in the early hours. I don't know what disturbed me, but I was now wide awake. Our cottage is an old building and I am used to the creaks and groans that come from it. But that night, all was still and quiet inside the building. Not a sound to be heard.

Outside was a different story, however. Our bedroom window is always open, and as I lay there in the moonlight, the outside night noises slowly made themselves heard.

The main noise was the sound of the sheep and newborn lambs up on the hill. I don't know whether the moonlight was keeping the lambs up, but there was a lot of baaing going on. It felt as if a group of Mums were calling their naughty children to order.

You could hear a lot of owls in the woods beside us as well. I don't know if their calls indicated good hunting or if they were just calling to one another. It was a very soothing sound though.

A pheasant called as well, and seemed very close. I was unsure whether it was in our garden, feeding off the birdseed scattered around, or whether it was an angry male trying to call a small harem to order.

Another bird called from down on the Saltings, and the cry was taken up by several other birds before they all settled back down again.

The whole thing was very soothing and seemed perfectly in accord with the scheme of things. Even a vehicle driving smoothly through the village seemed to add to the peace and quiet as opposed to disturbing it.

I snuggled down under the covers and settled back to sleep again; thankful that I live in the countryside.

Open Drains

Like many houses, we have a drainage system to keep the garden from flooding. Not a perfect system by any stretch of the imagination, our garden never really turns into a swamp as any rainwater is quickly sent on its way and conveyed down to the creek by centuries-old technology.

It is a different story with the gully that is just outside the garden.

This gully is fed by three overflow pipes that send water that has drained off the hillside above us onto a more direct route to the creek.

That is the general idea but it doesn't always work.

Frequently during the autumn the gully fills rapidly with the leaves falling from the trees above. Then when it rains hard and the overflow pipes work, the water pours into the blocked gully and rapidly backs up.

We are normally made aware of the blocked gully when the water starts streaming across the entrance to our drive and begins to flood our garden and the one next door.

This is the moment when you fully realise the flaw in the gully design: it lies completely open to the sky above.

As a result, at this time of year – it gets full of leaves.

At least one day a week I have to go out there with a rake and a pitchfork to clear the gully out. As I set to work clearing little dammed-up sections, the build-up of water behind rushes down the pipe and sweeps all sorts of muck down through the grille into the pipes beneath.

This is all well and good but my fear now is that one day the water will no longer flow away through the pipes as they will be blocked as well.

Then what am I going to do?

Sam and the Bluebells

What is it about the charm and beauty of a bluebell wood that attracts people so much?

As a youngster, back in the Fifties, there seemed to be a great sense of magic about such places. Bluebell woods always seemed to encourage thoughts of elves and fairy folk. I wouldn't have been surprised to have see a unicorn walk past, or a rabbit dressed in a new coat and trousers and staring at his watch.

There always seemed to be a stillness and great sense of peace in these places. In those days, we would happily walk around the woods and pick bunches of bluebells to take home to Mum. Thank goodness it is a practice that is now frowned upon today and is not allowed. We would pick armfuls of flowers which would sadly wilt and normally be discarded long before we got in a few hours later.

I now prefer to look at these plants in their rightful place and leave them for others to enjoy.

That glorious blue carpet that I remember being such a part of my childhood is now again on show as I deliver the post and along the lane by us. After work, I took my youngest grandson, Sam – 'I'm two and three-quarters, Grandpa' – along there for a walk.

It was amusing to see him dashing about and inspecting everything in the most noisy and busy way possible as we made our way along. It was also a real reminder of my own childhood to see him later sitting quietly amongst the bluebells.

Not making a sound, but with a real sense of wonder across his face, he just sat and gazed about him. Was he watching for a unicorn or a Cornish Piskey?

I'm glad the magic of these places is still there in the eyes of the young.

Our Well

The pump that empties our old well stopped working the other day. It had been playing up for a week or more and like the chap with a fading battery who just presses the switch even harder I pumped harder to get less water. In the end the water just ceased to flow.

I am no engineer and usually very clumsy with tools, but the thought of paying for the water to irrigate the garden instead of getting it free, convinced me to attempt to fix things.

Linda's face grew pale as I marched off with toolbox and drill; and got even paler when I proceeded to dismantle the pump. Thankfully, the modern world had provided me with 3-D plans of the pump via the computer; and the more practical and historical world provided me with a pump that did its job very simply and had few moving parts.

Even a numpty like me could take the pump apart fairly easily; and even I was able to see that the leather cup that provides the suction had perished beyond any saving.

I sat at the computer and duly ordered the part for the well and I pondered how amazing it was that they even sell things like that in the digital age.

A few days later the leather cup arrived and it was fitted in record time, by my standards. It actually took several hours because a kindly neighbour pointed out that it still wouldn't work unless I greased the leather cup thoroughly; and finding grease took ages.

I felt as chuffed as Moses hitting the rock, when I started pumping and the water flowed once more. A minor miracle.

A Four Season Day

A while ago, I experienced one of those days referred to as a four season day. By the time I had got to St Mawes sorting office and parked, the sun was glaring down at us from the other side of the harbour. With a promise of warmth for the day ahead, the sunlight was harsh to the eye as its rays beat down on us.

It was only later as we worked in our office that we noticed a change. The summer which started the morning had turned to autumn as a cold wind slowly picked up.

Dropping the temperature steeply, the wind had brought clouds scudding across the sky. Chilly now, and with a feeling of lowering cloud and a drenching to follow, the day had taken a turn for the worse.

Later still, as I got loaded up and ready to climb into the van, the first drops of wind-blown rain hit me in the face.

This seemed to be the pattern for the day ahead. Glimpses of sunlight and a nod in the direction of warmth, while at the same time, cold rain sweeping over us.

Not only was the rain cold but the wind constantly whipped it against my skin as I continued on my rounds.

It was hard to believe the day was still a part of springtime as these different weathers confronted me.

It was as I drove up a country lane and reached the top of the hill that the biggest shock was in store. Suddenly I was stuck in a blizzard of white that swirled across the front of the van and lay on the surfaces.

'Surely not snow,' I thought. 'Talk about four seasons in one day!'

Thankfully it turned out to be a blizzard of May blossom.

A Free Lunch

The poor blackbird must have flown into the conservatory window at some speed; it was obviously dead. I didn't like to leave it where I'd found it because I knew the children of the house would be home from school. I didn't want them upset.

With that thought I picked the body up and put it in the back of my van. It was some minutes later as I drove around a corner that I spotted a tiny figure in the road and braked hard. A small dark mouse was running away from me before it turned and launched itself at the grass verge. I moved forward and then braked sharply again as a flurry of feathers shot in front of me, before swerving up into the air and settling on a telegraph pole.

The buzzard and I gazed at each other... it was obvious I had disturbed its hunt for a juicy mouse. It looked at me, hoping I would move on so it could continue hunting. I looked at it and thought: I'm not leaving a little mouse to your beak and talons.

It was stalemate...and then I had an idea.

Quietly I climbed out of the van and went to the back door; opened it and lifted out the dead bird... I then held it carefully up in the air. The buzzard watched intently. Showing him the dead bird, I walked across the lane and placed the small body on a fence post.

I drove up the road and parked, watching carefully.

After a moment's careful checking, the hungry bird swooped down close to the dead bird and checked it all out. Obviously satisfied it flew onto the post and picked the bird up in its talons. It then flew off.

I think I did the right thing.

A Million Flies

Years ago, as a young Postie, I delivered mail to a fairly run-down property. The whole place was past its prime and in need of repair. I never saw many signs of life except for a tatty old collie who had long seen better days.

In a yard which consisted mainly of mud and dung, this dog was never clean. About him circled a million flies. His sad life consisted of sleeping in a doorway; or simply lying in the mud.

He may have been a working dog once but those days seemed long gone.

The smell off him was something else, as were the flies. Sometimes he was covered in stuff that defied description, other times he was soaking wet from the previous night's rain.

Every morning when I got there he would nose at my pocket and I would give him a dog biscuit. He always wagged his tail at me, and his sole surviving ear would prick up at my voice.

Then one day he was gone. I missed him and assumed he'd died. It was a couple of weeks later that the owner asked me had I seen the dog. Picking the sense out between the swear words, I understood that the dog had wandered away…and would not be missed.

A couple of months later, I started on another duty. This was about three or four miles away.

A small and tidy cottage on the new route had a wonderful elderly lady living in it. She had an old dog and introduced me to it. A clean, glossy-coated collie ran towards me, tail wagging, and pressed his nose up against the pocket I always carried the biscuits in.

His one ear pricked up as I gave him a biscuit. His secret was safe with me.

Acres of Sky

There are far more acres of sky above me since we moved to the south-west. I am enthralled on my deliveries when I look across to the west and see huge black clouds sweeping towards me. I can be walking in brilliant sunshine but I now have ample warning of a new 'weather feature' on the way.

The colours can be extraordinary as the sun shines on a darkening sky. The swirls and depths of the clouds are constantly changing, with occasional flashes of piercing light as gaps appear for the sun to peep through. Never has the phrase 'every dark cloud has a silver lining' been more appropriate.

Working along the coast gives you a glorious sense of the thousands of acres of sky above you.

Recently I watched in fascination as a furious black cloud invaded the blue sky above St Just. It swept across the Carrick Roads estuary and seemed to have me in its sights. Behind it was a strip of blue sky. The whole thing was like a forecast of the next hour or so.

The sky darkened swiftly and the hailstorm thundered down. Everything was cold and dark, and my shorts did nothing to protect my legs from the hail's sting.

Almost as quickly the cloud raced on and the blue section following behind gradually dominated the sky above me again.

The sun shone once more.

Unlike me, who had remained delivering outdoors, the more sensible of the community ventured back outside to resume whatever they had been doing. This seemed to include all the animals and birds in the area.

How lucky we are, with our vast, telltale sky, that we can see what's coming; can make plans accordingly; and can continue with our day relatively unscathed. Forewarned is most definitely forearmed.

Ambush Geese

I was ambushed by a flock of geese once. Everybody told me how clever they were to have worked out a method of attack like that. I confess the praise of these geese fell on deaf ears with me. My biggest concern by then was seeing the whole flock hanging up in some butchers shop somewhere.

At one of my calls, a couple of geese would always try to alarm me. They would lunge at me, hissing like snakes, and attempt to peck me good and hard with their beaks.

I would nip in and out of the yard at high speed, combining that with much arm waving and dodging about. It seemed to work and nothing harmed me.

Then one day it happened. A momentary lapse of attention, a moment's distraction, and one of them caught me. It was a combined peck and stab to the top of my thigh, and boy did it hurt.

Incensed, I spotted a lump of wood on the ground which I grabbed. Now armed, I turned and attacked the geese. They promptly ran off and I gave chase.

What happened next was best described by the owner of the geese who rang up my office to tell the manager. Imagine this being said down the phone by somebody laughing like a drain.

'I saw your postman pick up a lump of wood and start chasing the two geese. They ran off around the side of the barn. Your postman chased after them waving his lump of wood. They all disappeared. Then your postman came dashing back minus the lump of wood. Behind him was the entire flock of geese…there's twenty of them…they all seemed bent on catching him too. It's the funniest thing I've ever seen.'

I wasn't amused at all.

'Mummy's in the...'

I find young children refreshingly honest. 'They see it, they say it,' seems to be how they function.

'Mummy threw a plate at Daddy this morning.'

'Daddy fell over last night and hurt his leg. Mummy said it served him right.'

'My sister's having a baby.'

'The dog was sick on the carpet.'

'My Dad says... "Here he comes, a great big stupid grin on his face and a pile of junk to go through me letter box." He was talking about you.'

All these little snippets from the most honest members of my community are remembered if they are important; the rude ones never forgotten. A favourite of mine was the four-year-old who appeared in his garden clutching a letter.

'My Dad said this isn't ours... he said you're a prat. What's a prat?'

My answer was, 'Your Daddy was saying I'm just like him.'

I've no excuse: it had been a fraught morning, and thankfully nothing ever came of it. I imagine the nipper had forgotten our conversation and never mentioned it.

My most delightful piece of honesty came from a youngster and left me creased with laughter.

I got to a front door and rang the bell. I had a large parcel. The door slowly swung open and a little boy aged about three stood there.

'Hello,' says I, 'Is your Mummy or Daddy there?'

'Daddy's gone to work; Mummy's in the toilet doing a poo.'

A voice from behind the nearest closed door wailed, 'Oh no! I told you to tell him I was busy, nothing else!'

'Don't worry, love,' I spluttered with delight, 'I'll leave the parcel on the floor. Don't worry, I'm not embarrassed.'

'Oh, just go away.'

I have a feeling she wasn't happy.

Blue Skies

Have you ever noticed how perfect a bright blue sky is as a backdrop? It seems to complement every colour that stands up against it. Throwing everything against it into sharp relief, a tree always seems more of a tree; a cottage more of a cottage; a plant more of a plant.

I'm not even sure how to explain it really.

I glanced up at a small stand of trees, leaves shimmering in the sunlight. The darkness of the leaves contrasted sharply with the blue of the sky. Sunlight flickered on the leaves and it just looked so special, like a favourite moment captured as a photograph.

A cottage I delivered to later that day seemed to be at an angle with a lot of sky behind it. The white paintwork seemed to have softened into the walls, while the weathered old tiles on the roof glowed gently in the sunshine.

The whole combined to give off the air of a sleeping cat, dozing on a wall. The blue sky behind it seemed to cradle it into a general picture of contentment.

Again, later on, I drove past a field of bright yellow rape. It was as if I was driving past a sun lying on its back in a field. Glowing brightly, almost glaringly, it hurt the eye to look upon it. Glancing up at the edge of the field, the contrast between the bright yellow and the almost blue-black sky reminded me of the dazzle camouflage on ships in the Second World War.

Three separate pictures in my mind, each with its own unique set of colours and shapes; yet all enhanced in different ways by the blue sky behind.

The little wisps of white cloud added to it as well.

This really is a beautiful world.

Spritzer's Paw

Several years ago, a farmer I delivered mail to acquired a new dog. A small terrier, her job was to keep the rats down in the outbuildings. They called her Spritzer.

I don't know how good she was at killing the rats, but she tried to kill my ankles on a regular basis. The only defence I had was to face her; then she would back away only to try and sprint behind you so she could have another go.

Her other target wa the wheels on my van. What her thoughts were concerning the tyres, I will never know, but she declared war on them from the first time I drove into the farmyard.

A farm, by its very nature, is a busy place. There are tractors and machines which are not so much parked as abandoned. There are animals and fowls which seem to have less sense than they should have when it comes to vehicle movement. There are children, both young and old, who forget any thought of the Highway Code. And there are always the waste products which seem to lie everywhere.

You need eyes in the back of your head to negotiate and reverse in this farmyard without an 'attack terrier' joining in.

Several months later the inevitable happened. I didn't see Spritzer attacking a rear wheel... until she squealed in a most tragic manner... and I realised I had run over a paw.

I got out of the van but she limped away.

Ever afterwards, the dog still attacked my ankles, but never came off the porch steps when the van was there. As I reversed away though, until the end of her days, I swear she always slightly raised one paw and threw a reproachful look at me. She never let me forget.

Buzzard Playtime

I see lots of birds of prey in the course of my duties and they are a fine sight. There are kestrels hovering motionless in the air looking for dinner; falcons flying along keenly scanning the ground; and buzzards barnstorming across the sky.

The buzzards are my favourites as they slowly wheel and circle around the sky. They are majestic and have a cry that makes my blood tingle as they call to one another in the heavens. They are delightful.

Sometimes they come down to me and I catch glimpses of them flying from branch to branch, or flying away off a fence post as I drive by, or once or twice see them making a kill on the ground. The controlled power as they dive on something is breathtaking.

And one day a buzzard and I played a game.

Some years ago, as I drove along a country lane delivering mail, a buzzard swooped down in front of my van and seemed to invite me to play a game of tag.

Moving along at about thirty miles per hour we kept pace with each other. The buzzard flew about four feet off the ground, which put it squarely in front of my windscreen, and about a foot in front of the bonnet.

Twice he appeared to glance back over his shoulder as if to encourage me as he swooped and swerved across the lane. It was so exhilarating during the twenty seconds or so that he flew with me before, with a waving flip of the wing, he bade farewell and swooped over the hedge and was gone.

Cattle Grids

One of the cattle grids on my delivery got removed from the entrance to a property a while ago. Guarding a field which has long had no animals, the grid had become a bit of a waste of time.

Built when the property had genuinely been a farm, it had no function at all now except to startle the unwary. Over the years, the metal poles had gradually loosened over the pit so that driving over them resulted in a loud clatter and rattle.

On more than one occasion I have shocked people walking past as I exploded across the grid onto the driveway running through the empty field beyond.

Now the pit has been filled in, the poles removed, and all is peaceful.

It struck me though how different these grids used to be. As a postman, I have driven, ridden, and walked over many in my life. They have all served the same purpose, yet there have been many varieties. Some have been made of old railway lines, others strong scaffolding type poles, some have even been made of wooden poles like hop poles.

The pits too have been different. Some deep, some shallow; some brick, some concrete; even some full of water, others bone dry.

For me though, I have always classed the cattle grids in only two ways; those that are nature-friendly and those that aren't.

Some are just a huge trap for any unwary small animal, others are not. More and more now I see a slope built from the pit floor up to the top so any unlucky small animal toppling in has a means of escape. To me this is done as a kindness by thoughtful people. In the scheme of things, it may not be much, but I always feel better for seeing it.

Changes in the Countryside

Being privileged to work in the same piece of countryside on a daily basis, I get to see the changes made. Some happen quickly and often quite violently, while others are gradual and only noticed over time.

Whether the changes are wrought by nature or man, this applies to both. Trees felled by either chainsaw or high winds can leave a sudden gap in the landscape. A hollow in the ground can become a pond overnight; a small insignificant stream, a flood.

An empty field can suddenly fill with livestock at a moment's notice.

Then there are the more permanent things. The derelict barn or outhouses that slowly get converted into homes or workplaces; the unused field that finds a new use as a stable is built for ponies; a storage barn is built there for feed; or a shelter is built for cows or sheep.

Nature too, will suddenly find itself providing burrows and living space for rabbits, or badgers, or foxes. The trees fill with nesting birds that arrive as suddenly as they leave.

I enjoy continual flux the best. The wild flowers that appear, at their time, throughout the year; the trees that look dead in winter before suddenly greening over and looking so alive for the summer. Autumn colours come all too soon and then the trees sleep once more.

The farmers' fields are the biggest indicator for me. A lone tractor, with its attendant flock of seagulls, ploughing the field brown is followed by the slow days until the field greens over.

Steadily the crop grows stronger and greener before once more the colour changes, and it is golden. Great activity ensues before once more the field lies empty, its grey face stubbled as it rests.

Then a lone tractor turns it brown once more.

The same place; always changing. It's wonderful.

Chickens in the Garden

When I deliver the mail, I am finding that more and more people are keeping chickens in part of their garden. Some are in movable pens that are weekly moved around the garden to another spot; others are in permanent enclosures; yet others are allowed a free run of the garden itself.

I have found myself being chased out of gardens by angry cockerels...Lord knows what I did to upset them. I took a peck to the side of my kneecap once from an equally angry female. Indescribable pain but the reason for her attack was obvious; I had walked between her and her chicks.

And on more than one occasion I have nearly been trampled to death by a crowd of them who thought my delivery pouch was a bag of hen feed.

On the good side, I do have a near inexhaustible supply of reasonably priced eggs to choose from.

All this leads me to my dear old grandfather's chickens of yesteryear.

My Granddad discovered that my grandmother was terrified of live chickens. When he brought home a dozen, she told him she would have nothing to do with them. He simply nodded, smiled, and said, 'Leave it with me then.'

He then built a chicken run that went all around the hen house and also his shed which stood beside it.

The chickens were let loose in their new run and quickly made it their own. Granddad put an old armchair in his shed when Gran was out shopping one day.

The result was a small haven of tranquillity where he could hide out with a flask of tea and the newspaper. Poor old Gran couldn't go in because of the 'damned birds', and he swore he only turned his hearing aid off because the 'damned birds' made too much noise.

Cloud Gazing

Did you ever lie on your back in the grass and stare up at the clouds?

As youngsters, it was a favourite pastime, especially after a hard day playing in the fields. We would lie in the tall grass and stare up at the large blue bowl of sky above us and try to make shapes out of the clouds.

Each of us would point out various clouds and try to interpret the shape that we could see to the others. It could be a face, or a ship, or a car. Castles in the air.

We would lie there and imagine what it would be like to walk about on those clouds and gaze down on the world beneath. It was a well-known fact that angels used to sit on the big white fluffy ones and play on small harps.

If we were still full of energy, we used to race against the clouds' shadows that hurried across the ground. We would race ahead of the edge of sunlight moving towards us; or the edge of shadow and see if we could get into the shelter of the shadow of the trees on the field's edge, a great game which had us all laughing and gasping as we hurtled down the field.

I sat in my post van the other day drinking from a flask of coffee and looking out over a field towards Falmouth.

My running days are over as far as racing a cloud goes (perhaps), but I did gaze upwards and watch a face appear in the clouds and a castle appear just behind it. These are the times when you forget you are grown-up and you look at the world through the eyes of a child.

Cold, Crisp Mornings

Without a doubt, as winter settles in, the weather is changing. Gone are those happy, carefree days of summer with its warm temperatures, the occasional burning hot days when there wasn't a cloud in the sky, and the dust of dry ground.

Instead we are now greeted with damp, dank mornings; grey skies that are full of rain and keep the sun at bay; and wet, slippery ground that is neither pleasant or a delight.

We have rain pouring down on us; strong winds that are capable of knocking trees over; and chilling temperatures that could freeze the very soul inside you.

Then you get days like the one we had today.

There is a frost on the grass and the air is filled with the scrape of plastic on frozen windows.

The temperature drops further as a keen wind tries to cut you in two.

The sun rises slowly and reveals a sky of deepest blue with barely a cloud. It starts to produce some heat as it climbs into the sky and does its best to warm up the planet beneath.

Frost slowly melts and the temperature begins to show promise. We now end up with a crystal-clear sky, sparkly sea, reflected light that would dazzle you, and a barely perceptible heat that is at its best if you are out of the wind.

These are my favourite mornings. They carry a hint of all the seasons. There is a reminder of the summer gone; a reminder of the summer to come. They are a firm reminder that the winter is to be lived through; and enjoyed.

It is no wonder that these can be a postman's most favourite days.

Conned by a Dog

I am noted for carrying dog biscuits on my post round. It makes for an easier life sometimes. I have a collie on my round that gets a biscuit when I see him. A tragic creature, he lies quietly on a piece of matting beside the barn and contemplates life on the farm.

When I pull up in the van he slowly heaves himself up and turns a pained expression towards me. With an ungainly step, he limps towards me; his head is down; his body trembles with fatigue; he often collapses a few feet away from me and gazes with doleful eyes at the biscuit clutched in my fingers.

I admit to being very sympathetic with the dog and have often wondered why his owners should allow this wretched creature to suffer in their own farmyard. He always gets an extra biscuit... 'for his troubles'.

Then the other day I caught him out.

Arriving at the entrance to the farm I found the way blocked by a lorry. Nothing daunted, I walked the short distance down the lane and turned in through the gate. As I got there a sharp whistle rang out and I saw the old dog jump up. With an enthusiasm that astonished me, he dashed across the yard and chased the farmer who was riding a quad bike.

They both raced out through a gate and the dog overtook the bike as he headed for a flock of sheep on the hillside. Within minutes he had the sheep in a tight group and was bringing them back towards the yard. His energy was amazing!

The following day he once more performed his 'dying duck in a thunderstorm' routine for me. He looked quite shocked when he never got an extra biscuit 'for his troubles'.

Chickens and Eggs

Back in the Fifties, the farm we lived on supplied eggs to the Egg Marketing Board. My Mum and the lady next door were employed to collect, clean, grade, and tray the eggs. They would then load the trays into a very solid, huge cardboard box and a lorry would come to the farm and take it away. The box had green writing and a picture of a cheerful hen with a smiling sun beaming down on her.

In my entire life, that chicken shed has been the only place where I saw farming on an industrial scale. Certainly, it was the only place where I NEVER saw farm creatures allowed outside. I can picture it now...

The smell of that shed could knock you down. It was a combination of staleness, decay and bodily waste. It was disgusting.

Lights flickered in the ceiling to keep the darkness at bay. Not even one stray sunbeam ever reached inside the inner door, to alight on one of the cages.

The cages were stacked in rows, one on top of the other. As an anxious five-year-old I can vividly remember seeing the movement of what looked like a million de-feathered hens as they jostled constantly against each other. There always seemed to be one that was crushed and unmoving.

But it was the noise that was most sinister. It was either the deafening din as clucking hens were given food and water, whilst being robbed of their eggs; or the more gentle murmur as drowsing hens mourned a lost life in service to mankind.

I am told now that things are much improved and I hope they are right. Yet I can still see the picture on that box which bore no resemblance to the concentration camp within.

It was depressing and inhuman.

Cornish Hedges

I have never seen a hedge quite like a 'Cornish hedge'. Solid as a stone, probably because it is made of stone, it has a sense of permanence on the roadside. It is only when an unwary traveller pulls into the edge of the narrow road to let a tractor or lorry go by, and makes contact, that you are made aware of how unyielding it is. You only do that once.

It is hard to tell it's made of stone as it quickly becomes overgrown with greenery, while small bushes find narrow crevices filled with earth to take root and grow. It is only when you touch a Cornish Hedge that you get tangible proof of its solidity, and of the world of life it contains.

This diversity of plants and colour is never more profound than at this time of year when the daffodils are out. These hedges, which have stayed strong yet battered throughout winter, have just recently been covered in white from countless snowdrops. Now they are golden in the early spring sunshine with the inclusion of thousands of nodding daffodil heads.

On the Roseland there is a Cornish hedge that runs parallel to a road I use. The whole of the top of it is one long line of daffodils. The other morning in the gloomy grey mist which covered the road, they shone out like a beacon. It was beautiful to see.

Late afternoon that same day, I returned. The day had now become bright and clear; the daffodils had become like a long beam of sunlight pointing my way home.

I know that one of these days as spring turns to summer they will be gone and other plants and colours will take their place. And they will be just as beautiful.

Cows on a Hedge

I never give much thought to how big a cow is, or how heavy, until I am walking through a field of them; and never more so than when that field is full of both mothers and calves. Suddenly you then become very aware of the size of them. Especially if mother stamps a hoof on the ground or takes a step or two towards you.

Anxiety then creeps in as you look to see if you have walked between her and her calf. Is the cow feeling threatened by you? How did those horns grow ten foot wide and gain such sharp points? When did she grow to the size of a bus?

A cow lunged against me once when it was frightened; kicked its heels, and ran off. I lay flat on the ground as if poleaxed with a vision of a pair of hooves flashing over my prone head. I thought then that I knew how big a cow was.

The other day three cows decided to climb on top of a Cornish hedge, Lord knows how, and proceeded to chew the grass on top. I drove around the corner in my van and startled them as I drew up.

Two of them jumped straight back down into the field but the third slipped and teetered above me. It scrabbled and wobbled for a few heart-stopping moments right above my van, as it seemed to grow to the size of a small moon. I had visions of the poor beast crashing down onto the roof, or the bonnet, or me. Slowly it regained its balance before jumping down to join the other two. Just as well – the insurance people would never have believed that one: Postman Crushed in Van by Aerial Cow!!

Cricket in my Shirt

I seem to be more involved this year with insects and the like than ever before. I was asked to get rid of a large bumblebee the other day. Gently somnolent, it buzzed intermittently at a large window in a customer's house.

Believing bumblebees don't sting, I thrust my finger at it and allowed it to crawl into the palm of my hand. It sat happily as I got us both outside before it flew off onto a colourful plant.

No stings, so perhaps my old granny did get it right.

I continued on my rounds.

Within half an hour I had managed to walk straight through the biggest spider's web in the world. It felt very strong…yet it was almost invisible. If I hadn't caught sight of the giant spider that had woven it, I would never have known what it was.

A mesh-like web covered my whole upper torso and I had bits of it across my face, in my mouth and nose. My instant concern about the whereabouts of the spider was laid to rest when I spotted it swinging on a bit of web that was firmly attached to my hair. Thankfully the spider was now dangling at knee height and I was able to get rid of it.

I continued on.

Two hours later I was trying to prevent something scratching me. I thought a bramble had attached itself to my shirt until the itching moved across my back and suddenly got unbearable.

What people walking by must have thought as their local postman tore his shirt off in the village High Street I will never know…but I'm glad I did. Now all I need to find out is how such a huge cricket managed to get itself *inside* my shirt.

It was an unusual day.

Daisy Chains

It must be twenty years since I last saw anybody making daisy chains. I can remember my two daughters, Fiona and Lucy, sitting on our lawn and making chains for us all to wear. It kept them quiet and out of mischief for quite a time.

Their Granny had shown both girls how to make them a few days previously, and they were anxious to show us their new skills.

At the time I thought how strange it was that I hadn't seen any other children making these. At least, not since I had made them back in the early Sixties.

As children then who had with a lot more freedom than youngsters today, we would often spend all day out and about without parental interference. With no electronic games, mobile phones, or gadgets whatsoever, all activities had to be self-made, and, at the same time had to be fairly basic.

Burning up energy by dashing around, climbing trees, building dens, or kicking a ball about, was the usual game plan. Vast doses of imagination helped out with other games played. It was very simple to fight in a war, fly in a spaceship, or watch dinosaurs, so long as imagination was used.

There were times though when you just wanted to sit down and do something a little creative. That was when the daisy chain was brought into life. It was calming, restful, but at the same time, constructive.

At least you could see something for your efforts.

The reason I mention all this: the other day, as I walked up a garden path, two youngsters were sitting cross-legged on the lawn, busily making daisy chains of their own.

It was so unusual to see, and in moments, I was back on another walk down memory lane.

The Death of a Tree

I watched a tree fall over the other morning. In the high winds of the last few weeks it is inevitable that damage will result: garden furniture blown away and damaged; the odd loose roof tile or chimney pot smashed on the ground beneath; broken branches lying splintered on the road, with struggling leaves clinging to them.

The tree that I saw was a victim of high winds and the rain that had poured down the day before. It should not have been an exceptional tree, simply an ordinary tree standing on a bank with other, ordinary trees about it. What did make it exceptional however was that this tree chose to move and fall over.

For many years, it must have just swayed back and forth with all the others, doing what all trees do; then in a moment, it didn't.

This one tree seemed to shudder and tremble as if something had struck it a fatal blow. A branch swept around as if clutching at its trunk before slowly the tree continued to lean one way and topple over.

There was a tearing, cracking sound as if its very heart was being torn away and over it went. For a moment it looked as if some of the other trees were reaching out to offer support as their own branches tried in vain to stop one of their own from dying, but to no avail.

With all grace and majesty now gone, the once-proud tree crashed across the road and crumpled into the ground. It thrashed around for a breath or two and then lay silent and unmoving on the unyielding surface, its time over.

And all around, in the tempest, life continued.

Squeamish Postman

Many years ago as a young postman I overheard a conversation in our sorting office. It concerned the sad demise of a fine rabbit.

'It ran straight out in front of the van, Mick; didn't stand a chance. It's going in the pot later.'

'Where was that then, Bob?'

'Just up in Old Lane; I caught it with the front of the van. I stopped straight away and slung it in the back of the van in case anybody saw it. That'll please the missus; we're both partial to a bit of rabbit.'

And there the conversation ended.

Those of you who know me are well aware how squeamish I am. I eat meat but I couldn't kill anything and have been known to get really upset if I accidentally hit some creature and hurt it.

Thankful not to have been the driver who had hit the rabbit I carried on sorting and forgot the conversation. I was reminded of it later.

Mick and Bob left the office and walked up the yard. It was a few minutes later when Mick came in through the door laughing, and shaking his head. He called out to us all.

'That Bob's a soft eejit alright. We walked up the yard to his van and when we got close found his rabbit sitting up on the front seat and looking out of the window. He hadn't killed it at all…just knocked the wretched thing out.'

'So what's he done with it?' somebody asked.

'Poor old Bob, he's so soft; he said he couldn't kill it. He's driving back up to Old Lane to let the flaming thing go home. Can you believe the bloke?'

I did think, 'If he's anything like me, then yes, I can believe it!'

But with the other Posties, Bob never lived it down.

Disposable Waste

When I was young I would often take the dog for a walk. The instruction from my Mum was clear:

'Don't come home until it's done its business.'

Whatever 'business' the dog did remained in the place he left it, but I was under notice not to let him go on the pavement. In those unenlightened days, nobody dreamed of putting the dog's business into a bag and bringing it back home.

Nowadays we are much more controlled in what we do and nearly every dog owner I ever meet is always prepared with plastic bags, and other devices designed to keep the earth free of dog waste. With no embarrassment whatsoever, dog owners swiftly clean up after their pets; tie and seal the bag, and continue their way, bag in hand. The bag of waste is then deposited into the correct bin or taken home for disposal.

This is to be applauded and I in no way belittle these efforts.

But what sort of person feels it necessary to follow this sequence of events up to the bag-in-hand bit… and then chuck it up into a tree to leave it dangling off branches? Has anyone else seen these suspended parcels in trees and bushes all around the countryside?

Why all that effort to clear up, and then just abandon it?

I saw somebody, the other day, leaving a dog waste bag beside a fence post.

She told me, 'Don't worry about this bag. I don't want to carry it on the walk. I'll pick it up later when we return back.'

Half an hour later I was parked up on the top road and saw the same owner getting into a car with the dogs and driving off. It was obvious that owner and dogs had not 'returned past' as was said.

Sure enough, the bag was still sitting where she left it.

In a world where our countryside is a precious resource to be worked in and enjoyed, it is inconceivable to me that some folk feel that this is the way forward.

Donkey in a Field

There is a donkey on my round. As far as I am aware, he is the only donkey in a farm full of ponies. He has become a special favourite of mine.

Coming from an Irish background on my father's side, I was always aware of the donkey as a useful employee around the place. As a child on holiday at my grandparents', I would often see a donkey pulling a small trap along; or carrying turf in huge panniers for the fire; or just quietly letting life go by as it chewed on a thistle head.

However, as a young lad back in Surrey, where donkeys were few and far between, I sometimes found myself likened to a donkey more than once. I would behave as silly as a donkey; be as stubborn as an old donkey; or make as much noise as an old donkey.

I was told I lashed out like a donkey in a temper; brayed nonsense like a donkey; had big ears like a donkey; and even took 'donkey's years' to do the simplest of tasks.

This was the negative, but there was also the positive.

We were told stories of the wise old donkey to whom all the animals would come for advice: we were told by the old priest that the donkey had been present when the baby Jesus was born; had transported the family to safety in Egypt; and had carried Jesus into Jerusalem on Palm Sunday. And this was why he has a shape of the cross in the hair on his back; it's because he's special.

I see in the donkey a stoic, dependable, hard-working character, who if well looked after is totally at peace and comfortable with himself. Now that to me is also special.

Ducks on a Pond

I saw three ducks on a pond the other day while on my rounds. They cheerfully swam up and down a section of the water and seemed without care as they delved amongst the grasses growing up through the water.

Every so often, one of them would stop and nuzzle about a bit with its beak in the grass as if looking for food.

I couldn't help but smile at the antics of them, and tried to imagine the surprised looks they would have if they moved a little further out onto the pond, and then dipped below the water, as only a duck can.

This pond, as they would have soon found out, was not as it seemed. Certainly, along one side of the pond was a grassy bank and plenty of mud; but that was as natural as the pond got.

In every other way, it is a temporary puddle that lies across part of an old concrete road built by the American military in the 1940s. It is only this small section that floods, but it seems to happen after the smallest shower of rain.

With the rain we have had this winter it is hardly surprising that the puddle has grown to lake-sized proportions, which has included covering part of the grassy bank.

Those three little wild ducks were obviously delighted to have found a pond, seemingly free of any other ducks, and looking like it offered refuge and food.

Sadly for them, I fear all they would have got for their efforts would be a beak full of concrete, and the chance of being run over by the next vehicle to come along. Not quite the safe haven they were looking for.

Early Morning Harbour

I drive my van down the hill towards our small harbour at St Mawes. The early morning is one of my favourite times to be there. I have a permit to park on the harbour quay and I head straight for it.

In the summer months, the sun is always up over St Anthony Head and it reflects on the ever-moving water. On windless days the sea moves smoothly up and down, but on more choppy days it sparkles and glints in the sunlight.

Seagulls call loudly from the rooftops as they watch with a sharp and beady eye for anything they can swoop down on and eat.

When the tide is out it leaves a desert of sand and pebbles, with a collection of moored boats lying on the sand like discarded toys. The familiar blue and cream Falmouth ferry boat clings quietly to the harbour wall as it waits for its passengers.

Locals and holidaymakers are already about, all busy in their own little world. Most of them are getting papers from the tiny Post Office, plus bread and pasties from the bakery on the quay. The rest are having breakfast, or perhaps a coffee, sitting at the tables on the quayside itself.

In the winter months, the sun arrives a little later than me, but it is still just as nice there. The gulls still call although the pickings are slimmer. The boats are still moored in the sea although there are fewer of them. There are more locals now than holidaymakers, but they still carry on with the same early morning shopping.

Lighted windows beam in a friendly fashion from the shops, while that same old sea, more grey now than blue, slaps at the stonework on the quay.

And so my day begins.

First Full Day

I had a great day off the other day; I got called in for overtime. I was asked if I could help them out and do my own small duty before heading off and covering a duty on the nearby north coast. I couldn't resist. I was given a mail van, a real old bucket of bolts but it moved and that was the main thing.

I got my own duty prepared and delivered before being given a pile of packets and three bags of mail for the extra work and was pointed in the general direction of Perranporth. I had taken the precaution of getting myself an A to Z of Cornwall when we moved down here, so, with that opened out on the dashboard, I headed off into the late afternoon.

Our hero, i.e. me, neglected to take a torch so the last sixty houses were delivered in the dark. God knows what the customers thought as I blundered around the place like 'Blind Pew'. They must have thought an inept burglar was stumbling by. But I had a great time; my first eight-hour day since moving down to Cornwall.

A lovely lady saw me attempting to read the envelopes under a street light and loaned me a torch. I think the torch could have been used as a searchlight during the war, the beam was so powerful. It did the job though and I finished, with all mail delivered.

I know it can sound ridiculous but if anything has kept me working for Royal Mail, apart from the history of it, and the close group of friends I worked with, it is that great sense of achievement when you know you have delivered everything, and the customer has their mail.

Rural Economy

I have been struck by the level of honesty that goes with living in the countryside. As I drive my mail van through remote lanes and roads it is good to see signs of a thriving rural economy all about. All through the year I have seen fresh flowers and surplus vegetables for sale outside farm entrances or cottage gates. Whatever is in season at the time is proudly displayed for all to buy.

Throughout the year I can only guess that local chickens are contentedly, yet busily, laying eggs at a prodigious rate. At every turn there seems to be a small, handmade stall containing trays of goodies to tempt me and boxes of new-laid, free-range eggs. Not to be outdone are also the proud and confident jars of home produced jams and marmalades; even pots of golden honey.

There is something very satisfying about living and working amongst people who have enough respect for each other to make this economy work. There is the seller who is confident that people will pay what they owe without stealing; and the passer-by who is scrupulous enough to put the money in the box without a thought of just taking.

This is our very own Garden of Eden, and yet occasional problems still occur. In rural areas where we are all known to each other there are unhappy signs appearing. One chap found his eggs plastered along the cottage wall opposite. Yet another person left his wife's laundry basket outside which was full of produce. His hand-written sign said simply: 'Please help yourself: Donation in the pot for Help for Heroes'.

Somebody chose to take the first clause literally and lifted the entire basket into the boot of their car and drove off with the lot, including the basket. No donation.

It is still an honest place but every paradise has its snake.

Force of Nature

Once again, it has been brought home to us all just how insignificant we are in the violent face of nature. Torrential rain, powerful winds, and an implacable sea have shown us all that it is better to live with the elements than to fight them.

Rainwater has once again saturated our back garden and allotment. Although the surface water flowed down to the creek and did not cause actual flooding for us, in other parts of the south-west they have not been so fortunate.

Here high winds have had fun with the dustbins; have behaved like vandals with the bird feeders; and have decimated some of the taller plants still standing in our borders and pots. Once again we have been luckier than others who have seen structural damage to homes and businesses, never mind the number of trees uprooted and branches torn down.

However, it was the sea that reserved itself for the costlier damage. The sheer power of some of the waves was breathtaking. The ability of the tide to bring the sea into our homes and our streets was as humbling as it was unstoppable.

I was greeted in St Mawes as I collected the mail with waves coming over the sea wall, and water flowing backwards and forwards across the road. There were stones of every shape and size... everywhere.

If you timed the dash from van to office wrongly, the least you would get was a thorough soaking from head to toe. The worst you could get was a painful blow from a stone.

The worst I got, thankfully, was a cracked windscreen, although the cold soaking was a shock.

I for one have now learnt that nature must be respected. Our world, especially in the south-west, is beautiful... but we can never take it for granted.

Forty Shades of Yellow

Ireland has its forty shades of green; and the south-west seems to have its forty shades of yellow in the spring. In the last month or so out in the countryside there have been daffodils and narcissus showing every shade of yellow imaginable. From the deepest gold through to the palest, almost white. And don't these colours stand out against the green.

Now too, they are competing with the thousands of clumps of primroses, whose yellow faces almost glow, they are so bright. I have not seen so many primroses growing in the wild since I was a small boy back in the Fifties and Sixties.

This was a time when it was quite acceptable to pick as many wild flowers as you could manage and take them home. My Dad used to go one better and dig up whole clumps to replant in our own garden. Now it is important to just leave them alone on the banks of our lanes.

The gorse too has masses of golden yellow blooms smothering the bush and shining for all to see. It has amazed me to see just how many shades of yellow the gorse bush has as well.

Add to this the humble dandelion, which seems to be growing in even more profusion than normal, and you have a countryside bursting with yellow.

On the dullest and wettest of days, all these plants glow with colour, and on the occasional sunny day, they transform into glorious beacons of light.

After all the cold weather we have had, it has been a most wonderful and most colourful start to the spring. Yes, our countryside is mainly green and that is how it should be, but I never noticed until this year how much the yellow complements it.

It is a delight to the eye.

Game of Fetch

I am a great believer in animals sometimes feeling the need to play. They race around together; they mock fight; chase leaves; or simply find ways of driving their owners to distraction. I do believe that all play, for every creature, is simply a way to learn how to live by having fun doing it. It's nature's way of learning things, and play will stand you in good stead in the future.

There is a dog on my round that likes to play a game, and this game she seems to have taught herself. I have seen her playing it and I'm sure she is enjoying herself. No tail could wag so much without huge enjoyment.

Her name is Nell, she is a collie, and she has learnt how to play 'fetch' while playing on her own. I can guess how she learnt and to me, that is what life is all about.

She walks purposefully up the sloping drive towards the gate. In her mouth, she holds a disreputable-looking tennis ball. Nell arrives at the gate and turns to look down the drive sloping away from her. She then drops the ball and watches it bounce and roll down the tarmac and away from herself.

She allows it a head start before she gives a small bark and hares off determinedly down the drive to catch the ball. The small tennis ball is chased and harried before Nell triumphantly catches it, and returns back up towards the gate once more.

Then she does it all over again.

I know she is obeying every hunting instinct in her body to chase and catch her prey…but she has learnt how to play 'Solo Fetch'. And that really is clever.

Gardens through the Post

It wasn't until I became a postman that I discovered how much of people's gardens arrives through the post. A large chunk of mail delivered to the average door consists of gardening catalogues of one type or another. Bearing trusted names and displaying pictures of wonderfully colourful and immaculate gardens, they encourage us all to turn our own average open space into a horticultural work of art.

The days are gone now when I used to collect hundreds of letters from pillar boxes, each one addressed to the senders of these catalogues. Each envelope would contain the order form, plus cheque, which would transform their plot.

Nowadays the internet is kept busy as order forms and cash whizz silently through the air...but the outcome is still the same.

Packets of seeds soon rattle their way onto my delivery frame. Even bags of bulbs come along, in their plastic netted containers. Boxes of small plants with their roots firmly placed into a pocket of soil come into our system by the van load.

On the odd occasion a small tree complete with large pot will wobble in through the door and wait impatiently to be planted. I have lost count of the bags of rose bushes (a stick with roots at one end and a leaf at the other) that have marched in as well.

All show a colourful description or photograph of the end result.

These are all delivered promptly to delighted customers who disappear excitedly with their prizes. Their new garden has arrived!

It must work, because throughout the year, I watch the gardens transform into colourful, even if not so immaculate, copies of the catalogues.

It's an odd way of gardening... but it does work and I'm glad to be part of it.

I just feel something is missing, that's all.

Dog Sense

I was told repeatedly as a boy that the most intelligent dog in the countryside is always the Welsh Border collie. I never saw any reason to doubt this over the years.

I would go to sheepdog trials or dog agility events, I would even watch *One Man and his Dog*. I never doubted the collie's intelligence and recently I witnessed a prime example of it.

A farm I used to deliver to has had a problem with the new countryside problem – 'If someone can steal it, they will'.

To combat the theft of fuel and equipment, the farmer has bought a guard dog. I was warned about it by the farmer who told me, 'It could rend you apart'.

Obviously looking worried at this news, I was assured that the dog would be locked up in the conservatory during the day, so I could just put the mail through the conservatory letter box. Further to the farmer's efforts to reassure me, it was also pointed out that I needn't worry if the door was open, as the guard dog would think it was closed and not get out at me.

These words of comfort fell on very disbelieving ears.

Some weeks later I found myself at the farm again. As I walked from the van, his friendly old collie came up, greeted me, and then walked beside me towards the conservatory.

I had already decided that before I stepped past the barn into the yard, I would peer around the corner and check if the conservatory door was shut.

I duly peeped around the corner before venturing forth, and couldn't help but chuckle. At my knee height, the collie had also stopped and was also peeping round the corner at the door before he, too, ventured forth.

Now that's what I call an intelligent dog.

Gull and a Golfball

The other day I drove into a customer's driveway and braked hard as a golf ball landed just to one side of my van. It bounced on the tarmac beyond and landed in a flower bed. Startled by this and assuming somebody in the village was whacking golf balls around, I looked out of the mail van window.

Debating whether to get out of the van or not, I saw a large herring gull fly down and advance on the ball. It looked at it in a puzzled fashion before picking it up in its beak and flying up on the garage roof.

The gull steadied itself before tilting its head back as far as it would go. He paused for a moment before snapping his head sharply forward and down. The gull then opened his beak and watched in some surprise as once more the ball cracked down hard onto the drive before bouncing up in the air and landing in the garden again.

The startled bird then walked down the slope of the roof and peered again with a confused look at the golf ball.

In great puzzlement, the bird flew down once more and proceeded to poke at the golf ball before finally admitting defeat and flying away. It circled over the ball before disappearing over the roof tops.

Grabbing the mail, I stepped into the garden and picked up the golf ball. It looked brand new. I know the man of the house plays golf so I put the ball on the window ledge in his porch, wondering: is it possible that the gull thought it was an egg and was attempting to break it for a meal?

Hanging Baskets

As a child I used to hear stories of The Hanging Gardens of Babylon. What had they looked like, I used to wonder? I would imagine great walls of stone festooned with a waterfall of green foliage, and mixed with flowers of every shade and hue.

I would envisage great shelves of level rock that could be walked on, with plants cascading down from the edges to other levels below. I just knew the gardens would be beautiful.

It is not too hard to imagine these ancient wonders when you see some of the gardens lovingly maintained in our West Country villages and towns.

With so many properties built stacked on top of each other down here, it is inevitable that some gardens are more perpendicular than they are level. To see a house chimney pot practically level with the neighbour's front door, shows just how building along contours creates these gardens.

Each individual property seems to do its best to outdo its neighbours; and this is achieved with ingenuity and with great determination. I imagine telling these homeowners that 'You can't' is probably all the spur they need to show that they can.

For those with more level properties, the hanging basket is probably the best way of emulating the hanging gardens. Wherever I look– and our own garden is no exception – the hanging basket fills a space.

There is a beauty about these baskets. Hanging from wall or ceiling, each one is its own little world of plants; both upright and dangling. They are vibrant with colour and life, breathtakingly gorgeous, and stand out for all to see.

Which is why I have never managed to explain just how I seem to hit my head on at least one basket a day when on duty.

Heron on the Beach

There was a heron on the beach the other day. It surprised me a bit as I think of herons as inland birds. Over the years I have grown used to seeing them standing beside rivers and lakes. I have watched them stalk carefully into the water and pause, only a sharp beady eye moving slightly as they wait for the right moment. Then a strike! and a luckless fish becomes a meal.

On various post rounds, I have seen whole fishponds in gardens emptied by a single voracious heron. Folk seemed powerless to stop them.

I only ever saw a heron beaten once. An old gardener told me that a heron will not land in the water. It has to land beside it and wade in. He ran a thin wire around the edge of his pond about a foot or so off the ground. This stopped the heron from moving to the edge to fish. It did work.

Then I saw a heron on the beach. Confident and unmoving, it stared rigidly into a large rock pool, waiting to strike. Suddenly, out of the early morning sun, swooped three seagulls. Like three feathered spitfires, the gallant few hurled themselves, diving in formation, at the heron.

Startled, the now ungainly predator flapped slowly up into the air. Although dwarfed by their adversary, the seagulls continued to swoop and dive as they harried the great bird. Screaming and crying they slowly forced the great bird off the beach. It repeatedly tried to turn back to the rock pool, but to no avail. Giving up, its powerful wings beat harder as it turned and headed back inland to safety, humiliatingly beaten.

I swear as the three gulls zoomed back triumphant over the beach, one of them gave a victory roll.

Honeysuckle

Suddenly, I am noticing honeysuckle everywhere. I love the cycle of life and growth on the banks and hedges beside our lanes. Not so long ago the hedgerows looked gnarled and stark; the only spark of colour was the little groups of berries to be found amongst the branches. There was some green, but not a lot.

Then the hedges slowly took on their springtime appearance and the daffodils arrived. For several weeks, the sides of the roads were a mass of different shades of yellow.

Since then, the hedges have darkened into summer green and a multitude of other plants have exploded onto the banks. These plants have been so varied in colour that the banks and hedges have taken on the look of a rainbow.

And now the honeysuckle has arrived and is perched on top of the hedges or cascading down the sides. Like a 'throw rug' that people drape over a sofa or favourite chair, the honeysuckle looks as if it is casually, yet artfully, thrown over the hedge.

As a plant, I have always thought it looks both hardy and at the same time, fragile. It has a beauty of its own. The stems, clinging to whatever it can hold on to, show a quiet determination to survive in any conditions. The simple, yet ornate flower with its delicate colouring and tube-like shape, seems so delicate for a plant growing in a hedge. It is a plant that seems to combine both strength and elegance at the same time.

Yet it is the scent that takes your mind to other places. As that wonderful perfume drifts across your senses, it brings a reminder of childhood. A reminder of when you were small; of when you were cocooned in love and safety; a reminder of your Mum.

Nuisance Caller

We seem to be having an early morning visitor to our cottage these days. He has gained the habit of knocking on various windows around the house.

The first time he came, he tapped vigorously on the glass of the front door. I went downstairs, giving a grumble about early callers on my day off, but found no one there.

I got back upstairs only to hear tapping on the back window at the kitchen. Once more I went downstairs to find nobody around. I ended up outside in the garden in a dressing gown and a pair of old gumboots, wandering around... but there was no one to be found.

I made my, by now, fully-awake wife and myself a cup of tea and returned to the bedroom. We were sipping the tea when we heard the tapping once more.

This time it was on the window of the spare bedroom upstairs.

The tapping was insistent, and guessing nobody standing in the garden could reach that high, we both tiptoed along the landing and peered around the half open door to the bedroom window.

There on the window ledge, and tapping for all he was worth with his beak, was a large herring gull. We stepped into the room and he caught sight of us. For just a moment he fixed us with a baleful eye before flying down into the garden and landing under the empty bird feeders. He then looked up at the bedroom window, before looking at the ground with a resigned air.

He must have got used to the smaller birds eating from the feeders, and worked out that any dropped seed could be picked up by him.

With no food spilling down, he had decided to bring this oversight to our attention.

Cheeky beggar.

Landslip

I witnessed my very first landslip the other day. Like most people, I often see the aftermath of a cliff fall or collapse of something, but I never actually see it happening.

This was a small one in a driveway on my delivery. As I turned the corner of the lane, I watched in surprise as part of the Cornish hedge in front of me just started toppling onto the driveway. I was moving towards it slowly and stopped the van.

At this point my first thought was probably the most obvious: how much of this is going to give way? This was closely followed by: what caused that to happen?

I stepped out of the van and took a closer look. I have to confess that nothing stood out as being a cause. We had suffered a lot of rain over the days before so I assumed that could have been a contributor. However, that day was dry and I couldn't see any dampness moving on the scar of earth left behind.

The rest of the Cornish hedge seemed pretty solid but I was reluctant to put it to the test by touching it. This was only a five-foot-tall hedge so I felt quite safe, even though I would rather not be buried underneath that much stone and earth if I could avoid it.

What did strike me though was how frightening it must be for someone caught up in a really big fall. Its suddenness catches you completely unawares; what was once solid and secure is now fluid and engulfing; and if you are in it, you are in deep trouble.

It was only a little fall and nobody was hurt, least of all me. However, just for a moment I have to admit, my instinct was to run away.

Spring Lambs

As I go on my rounds, I have been lamb watching over the last few weeks. A flock of mothers, all of them seeming to have two lambs each, have been using a field nearby.

Each day as I have driven by in my van, the young and unsteady lambs have raced off to stand beside Mum. They have watched anxiously from the safety of their mother's side as I have slowly driven past. I felt guilty causing such fear.

Now several weeks on, things are very different.

The mothers lie or stand around in the field, each busy, each indifferent to anything. Beside them, and also lying down or grazing, are a few of the lambs. I can't help but think of these lambs as the girls.

However, on the side of the field nearest the road is another group of lambs that I cannot help but think of as the lads. They hang around in a group and do their best to look menacing as I go past. On occasion, they throw caution to the wind and push and shove each other before all turning and dashing alongside the fence to the end of the field. They then turn around and pause, before hurtling back towards my van. Then they stop and stare at me once more.

Their behaviour then gets even more laddish, and after a quick glance towards the girls, they begin to strut and swagger about with the occasional head butt or rearing up thrown in.

Although keeping half an eye on proceedings, the girls tend to ignore the lads and their efforts to impress.

I smile as I remember how much this is just like the behaviour I used to be part of in the playground of my old primary school.

Like a Millpond

I've always liked the phrase, 'like a millpond'. It conjures up an image of calm and stillness that is hard to find. Often surrounded by trees, the pond rests quietly in its hollow, holding itself in readiness for the job ahead.

It is only when a sluice gate is opened that any movement is discerned; and even then it is only in one place where the mill race feeds the huge wheel on the side of the mill.

The rest of the time the placid water just lies there reflecting the world around it. There is an enchanted peace about this body of water that comforts a tired soul or body.

It's a balm; it can make you relax; it can make you pause; and it can make you happy.

I heard the phrase used the other day but it didn't refer to a pond or a lake; it referred to the Carrick Roads water between Falmouth and St Mawes. A normally very active piece of water, it constantly moves up and down as wind and tide keep it busy; but not so the other day.

I deliver the mail alongside it. When I arrived, a light mist rested across the water which gave it a mysterious, delicate quality. The wind had dropped completely and the whole area was still.

The water rose and fell, but with a gentleness that barely rippled the sea; as if the moon had fled earth's orbit and the sea had decided to have a lie-in.

A lone fishing vessel hauled up some crab pots; she barely made a ripple herself as she slowly meandered across the water.

Nobody could ever mistake the Carrick Roads for a millpond. But in that moment of peace and quiet, it definitely came close.

Litter Louts

Many years ago now, I lost my little sister just before Christmas. A moment's inattention; a big car; a six-year life over before it had properly begun.

Months later, my Dad sorting out some of her coats discovered that the pockets were full of cigarette butts.

It was drummed into us as children to always take our litter home with us. Susan had gone a step further and was picking up and taking home other people's as well.

Fifty-five years later and I find myself doing the same thing.

In my mail van I carry a box. As I deliver my letters I gradually fill it with the rubbish that people throw away. When I get back to the Post Office I place the recyclables in the correct bins and the rest into a dustbin.

What is it, I wonder, that makes folk think throwing rubbish into the hedges and lanes is a good idea? Glass bottles, metal cans, plastic everything, carrier bags... it's everywhere. Most of the rubbish is food and drink containers.

At a guess, I would assume most of this rubbish is hurled from the windows of passing cars. You have to wonder why the driver or passenger finds it so difficult to take their stuff home.

The other day though, a new level was reached. Some driver collected up all the rubbish in his car and put it into a carrier bag to get rid of it later. That later turned out to be 'getting rid of it' into the field beside the lay-by just outside St Mawes.

I jumped over the gate, dodged the cows nosing at the bag, and retrieved cans, glass bottles, and plastic containers before any injury could be sustained by the animals.

Why is it a six-year-old could do better than this driver?

Long Gardens

I read an article several years ago which went on at great length about the wonder of the unspoilt miles of untouched wilderness on the sides of our motorways.

They were described as being similar to nature reserves in as much as nobody stops alongside to disturb anything. Hedgehogs are thought to have evolved the ability to run from danger instead of curling into a ball; foxes and badgers have been filmed watching the traffic before dashing across the carriageway as soon as there was a big enough gap between the vehicles; flowers grow there in great profusion.

On my own country delivery, the nearest I get to a motorway is the main road leading into St Mawes. Quietly indifferent to the motoring world, it is fed by some extremely tiny and even more unspoilt country lanes. I swear it would be possible, and perfectly safe, to stop on one of these lanes and lay out a picnic.

Where the St Mawes road is similar to the motorway, though, are the miles of flowers and grasses growing along the edge of its surrounding lanes. Like extremely long and thin gardens, these lane edges teem with the most incredible plant life.

There are grasses of every shape and size, too many to identify, which fill these borders. Mixed in amongst these are all sorts of colourful plants. There is cow parsley in the greatest profusion, which this year seems to be vying for space against the beautiful campion.

Contrasting sharply with the purple of the campion is the white of dozens of daisies and the yellow of hundreds of buttercups. Bluebells too, seem to be growing wherever they can.

These self-maintaining gardens seem so much more magnificent when compared to the more formal gardens we design for ourselves. I love them.

Milk Churns and Platforms

I used to love seeing milk churns waiting on their platforms at the side of a farm gate or building. The old platforms were made of whatever material the farmer chose to use but they had to be strong enough to take the weight of half a dozen full milk churns, plus the weight of the man shifting them.

Our driver was called Wally and he would turn up twice a day at each platform, from the local dairy. As if by a miracle to my childish eye, every platform was just about the correct height for his lorry. Wally would open his door and swing himself onto the back of the flat bed of his lorry. He would walk across to the churns and step onto the platform.

Grasping the top of the first churn he would tilt it slightly towards himself and roll the bottom of it onto the lorry and across to the other full churns. Back and forth he would go rolling the full churns into place. He would then grab the empty churns on his lorry with the farm name on them and carrying one in each hand, swing them back out onto the platform.

Leaving receipt and signature behind, he would swing back into the cab and drive off to the next farm. While other boys wanted to be a train driver or a soldier or a pilot, I always wanted to have Wally's job.

In some rural areas, the old platforms are still there to see as I do my post rounds, although the house is now a farmhouse in name only. The churns are now some sort of rural antique; some are used as letter boxes but mainly as garden ornaments. But I remember cold winter mornings and soft summer evenings; churns and platforms; and Wally with his lorry.

Night Visitor

We took advantage of a long weekend off and went camping for three nights down near St Just in Penwith. A small campsite gave us an ample opportunity to get close to nature. We never guessed just how close we would get.

Normally we are in the habit of washing up and putting our things away. On this evening, however, we left everything in the washing up bowl and decided to clear up in the morning. The bowl was left under the stand that holds our small camping stove. Hanging from a hook beside the stove was a plastic bag with our waste food and rubbish. This bag was about 18 inches above the washing up bowl.

Silence settled and all was quiet in our little world. Just as I was drifting into sleep I heard a rattle from outside the tent. It sounded like a piece of cutlery shifting...all was quiet for a moment...and then I heard it again; this time followed by a crashing sound.

Both of us now fully awake, I leant across and fearfully slid the zipper up on the tent. We both gazed out...nothing.

Then we saw movement beside the washing up bowl. Linda shone the torch and two bright eyes glittered back at us. Delighted, we watched as a hedgehog was picking itself up. Using the washing up bowl and its contents as a ladder to reach the bag of waste food had not been the little creature's brightest idea.

It's been ages since we saw a hedgehog. Where have they all gone? Years ago, as a young postman, in the early mornings I would see hedgehogs as much as I still see foxes, rabbits, badgers and deer.

This was the first hedgehog in a long time; and even he ran off.

Nimby

There is so much argument these days about change. It seems that whenever anyone tries to do something different it immediately brings out the best and worst in people.

Mention of having a windmill erected on a bit of farmland; a tree needing pulling down; a path being rerouted; or even a house being painted an unusual colour. Outrage!! Don't even mention a new road or rail route. And certainly never even hint at a power station or perhaps an airport. More outrage!!

All these things result in battle lines being drawn up and everyone will have an opinion.

Our countryside either gets pickled in aspic where it can vegetate in peace, or it can continue to grow and move forward.

I read an article the other day concerning a railway viaduct.

Built in the early Victorian period to carry a railway line, it evoked outrage and protest from all in sight of it. A blot on the landscape; a danger to the farms and their livestock; it'll damage the river and its environs; we've had this view for centuries: the negativity rolled on.

Even so, the viaduct was built and carried trains right up until the Beeching cuts. It brought jobs and a living to many.

Then the railway offered to take it down as it was now redundant. More outrage and protest from all in sight of it. It's a wonderful example of Victorian architecture; it enhances our farms; the river flows gently under it; it's been part of the view for centuries: the positivity rolled on. The viaduct was spared and is now an integral part of a beautiful walking and cycling network. It brings jobs and a living to many.

I suppose it's what you're used to. It did make me think though.

Open Views

Have any of you noticed how open and beautiful our countryside looks in the winter? I never realised until I stood recently on the side of a hill above a river.

All through the year, I have only caught glimpses of what lay the other side of the trees. I could see the occasional glitter of the water as a wave caught the sunlight. A part of a wall or roof sometimes came into view, or the rare column of smoke from a chimney rose, almost vertically, into the sky.

All these things were largely hidden away by the leaves.

Now suddenly, with bare sleeping trees in front of me, I am aware of the houses beneath me and the river beyond. Each house I could identify as places I have delivered to, but I was looking at them from a different viewpoint.

The river too, suddenly seemed so much bigger as I could stare, almost uninterrupted, towards the banks and fields on the far side. Until that moment, I had been unaware that the boatyard I delivered to curved around towards a small lagoon, beside the now visible church.

The fields stretched away from me towards the horizon. Some were empty, while others had sheep, cows or horses in them. I had no idea that this livestock was there as, when I deliver over there, the surrounding hedges are too thick and high.

A voice broke into my thoughts.

'This is the best thing about the winter', he smiled, 'It becomes a whole different world when the leaves fall off the trees.'

He was quite right of course. My familiar surroundings were still familiar; but it had become a different world now the leaves had gone. I do love these changes but I'm glad they're not permanent…

Never Went Shopping Together

I used to deliver to a lovely old couple. They lived in a small village several miles from a big town. He had worked for the bus company all his life and had been conductor on the village bus until retirement.

She had been the only person working at the small railway station that served the same village. In her job she had worn many hats.

Childless, their whole world revolved around the village, their productive cottage garden, the countryside and their work. Their cottage had no mains water or drainage...but it had electric.

When I met them in the early 1980s they had both been retired for many years. They still didn't have a TV set, but both listened avidly to the radio and their old record player. Neither of them was much over five feet tall, yet both of them stood tall in the village, with regular prizes to both in the village fete She was a stalwart of the WI; he played darts regularly at the old station pub. Neither of them drove.

Both proud, they rarely asked for anything: they were already an anachronism in the 1980s, and we loved them.

They always made us chuckle on a Friday.

This was the day they did their weekly shop in the town, using their country, canny nature to save a penny. When he retired he'd been given a bus pass for life; when she retired she was given a train pass for life.

You can guess the rest.

Every Friday she would get on the train; he got on the bus. They would meet up in town and get the shopping, divide it between them, and return to the village the same way that they left it.

Thrifty, sensible...it brought us all amusement.

Overgrown Lanes

Have you noticed that the lanes are getting narrower? There always comes that time in the year between winter and whenever a tractor comes along with its mower attachment, that the banks look at their best. Overgrown with grasses and a multitude of colourful flowers, they are a delight.

Foxgloves strain lofty and tall on the banks, seemingly anxious as they wait for industrious bees to climb into their flowers. Campion too jostles with tall grasses as it pokes itself out into the sunlight. Even the humble 'cow parsley' has its place as it stands strong and proud, and seems to wave after every passing vehicle.

As you walk past with the overhanging foliage brushing against your legs and waist you can hear the murmur of insects and the scratching sound of some small creature hurrying secretly by. No wonder there are hawks hovering overhead.

I know that for safety's sake it is a priority to trim all this back and keep it tidy, but it is still a shame when it's cut. While it is left alone and untouched, it becomes as much of a jungle as you would find in any equatorial country.

With its impenetrable foliage, its carnivorous and vegetarian wildlife, it can be as wild and as beautiful as the Amazon basin or the Congo.

At the moment on some of our lanes, the grass is brushing against both sides of the post van at the same time. I feel like a fox or a badger as I move quickly through this trail of mine. I seem to have become as invisible to the world as those animals do. The overgrown lanes have become a secretive place to me, full of hidden dangers and perils, but they also feel like home.

Palm Trees

There is something exotic and mysterious about the palm trees that grow at the British seaside. They look foreign yet also look as if they belong, and they certainly enhance the feeling of being away on holiday for visitors.

There are several of these trees around the little church at St Just-in-Roseland, and they look as if they have belonged there for years. I normally park my mail van and have my meal break at the café beside the church under the trees. There are also facilities in place for the euphemistically styled 'comfort break'. But more importantly, it is also a lovely tranquil place to stop for a moment for a recharge of your own batteries.

The palm trees share the ground with the more usual native trees such as oak and ash, beech and pine. Like immigrants and native population, each complements the other if allowed, with the deciduous trees providing a sense of timeless stability and the palms providing the flamboyant exotic note. There is no nicer view of a bright blue sky, than when seen through the branches of a tree. The bark and the leaves seem to be clearer when pressed against a backdrop of blue sky.

Our quintessentially British trees rustle in the slightest breeze and seem to be whispering softly to a hard-of-hearing mankind. The palm trees also rustle in the breeze and murmur.

I can see no dates or bananas or coconuts in these palms but I can see the blue of the sea and the green of the fields behind them, just as I can with the native trees. They are foreign and exotic to me, yet, with what they bring with them, and with their own particular way of fitting in, they somehow belong.

Pheasant in the Wind

The other day on my post round, the wind was ferocious as it punched in from the sea. I watched as various birds fought hard to make headway and I was amazed at their persistence.

Very few of the smaller birds had ventured out that I could see, but some of the bigger ones were doing their best. I watched as a seagull, wings beating, was slowly driven backwards across the sky. It suddenly turned and swooped down at frightening speed and disappeared behind a hedge. Moments later I watched a crow seem to simply fold up and drop out of control into a field.

They looked battered and bewildered and reminded me of a pheasant I saw once on a similar day. We had been trail walking in violent weather and watched as a pheasant took off straight up into the wind. He had been proudly puffing his chest out and squawking and flapping as if lord of all he surveyed.

Wings beating furiously and body almost upright in the wind he then struggled to make progress. The wind simply pushed him backwards and, although his wings carried on beating, he remained upright as he slowly got pushed forty or fifty yards backwards. Still flapping and still upright he 'reversed landed' into the grass.

It had been amusing to see the astonishment on his face as he had flown backwards and landed, but we couldn't help but laugh out loud minutes later, as he trudged past us, head down and cheeks red, as he walked to his destination.

The poor creature stumbled on hurriedly, refused to look at us and disappeared quickly through the hedge, giving a perfect impression of total embarrassment. Even in nature there seems to be such things as pride coming before a fall.

Picking Wild Flowers

Are there any rules and regulations on the picking of wild flowers?

As with Health and Safety, one wonders if half the rules we abide by these days, are done so through fear of breaking a rule that exists only in somebody's mind.

I am told I must never pick a pebble or rock up off a beach for fear of censure…then the sea throws tons of the stuff over the road and in gardens for anybody to deal with.

It's difficult to cut a tree down that stands on your own property, even if it is rotten and liable to fall and cause harm at any moment, or so I am told.

All of which brings me back to my original question. One school of thought has me convinced that picking a wild flower will have me incarcerated in the Bastille. Yet I have been told in no uncertain terms that this rule only applies to the digging up of wild flowers, roots and all.

Knowing that ignorance is no defence in law…or so I've been told… I have ignored the voice in the back of my head that says, 'Linda would love a bunch of wild flowers.'

But not the other day.

The bank along the lane was so overgrown that it was being trimmed with a huge hedge cutter attached to a tractor. My logic dictated that these plants would be history in a few minutes' time. With this thought in mind I stopped the post van and picked a huge bunch of different flowers and grasses before annihilation stepped in.

The resulting bunch of wild flowers sits proudly in a vase on our table to Linda's huge delight. The chopped-down hedge cutter trimmings are quietly composting along the lane. No laws broken…I told myself.

Playing Shadows

I don't know where my mind went the other day but I found myself playing 'shadows' on my rounds. This was a game we used to play when I was young and enjoying the delights of the school holidays.

There was a huge recreation ground behind our houses known as 'The Field'. This was where we spent our days, and we loved it. Surrounded by trees, it was a wonderland for young children.

The game of shadows had very simple rules. The idea was to get across the field without stepping on a complete piece of sunshine. So long as you had a bit of shadow under a foot, this was considered a safe step.

We would spend ages trying to cross the field using the shadows of the trees as 'safe steps'. This worked perfectly until you came to a gap in the tree line. Then you had a choice: retrace your footsteps and try another way, or perhaps wait for that little cloud to cover the sun and make a dash for it.

I lost count of the times we would be halfway across a large patch of cloud-shadowed ground when the sun would burst through. This was instant death and you were required to fall flat on the ground while your mates continued with the game.

So there I was, on my foot rounds a couple of days ago, when I found myself deliberately stepping on shadows and zigzagging up towards the front door. A little jump got me safely into the porch and I smiled as I pushed the letters into the box.

I turned and was greeted by a smiling elderly lady coming out by the hedge. She grinned and said, 'I've just caught you playing shadows, haven't I?'

Blushing furiously, I had to agree. I did feel a fool.

Rustic Gate

I found a gate the other day which I didn't even know was there. A lane I drive down to deliver to an elderly couple is bordered on both sides by hedges. These are not your typical 'Cornish hedges' as there is no stone involved.

Comprising mainly bushes and small trees, these hedges are as organic as they come and are full of colour and life throughout most of the year. The growth is quite thick and tangled and would keep any animal enclosed. In front of both hedges is a continuous grass bank which is slightly higher than the road.

Looking solid and dependable, there is no way through the hedges along that lane.

I stopped the other day to pick up a couple of empty beer bottles which had been tossed on the verge. I always carry a box in the back of my van for anything that I can recycle, or anything I can put in my own dustbin when I get home.

As I bent down to pick the bottles up, I noticed something square and solid in the hedge. It turned out to be a gate post. Not only was there the post, but hanging onto it was a long five-bar gate. I looked further and noticed the gate was securely fastened to another gate post by a latch.

This old rustic gate must have been hung there at one time to allow access or egress from the field behind. No longer in use any more as a gateway into the field, it had been allowed to remain as part of the barrier.

Eventually the hedge had grown over it and around it, before finally absorbing it. The gate was almost invisible.

Built to do a useful job, it seemed strangely forlorn as it hung there...abandoned.

Pots and Kettles

Now that the hedges have lost some of their leaves I can get quite good views into fields and gardens I had never seen before. Some of these hedges have been there for a long time. It is possible to see small paths running both through and along the hedge; a testament if nothing else to the safety factor of the hedge for our smaller fauna.

I can also get a good view of things like an old five-bar gate that has become part of the hedge. Another hedge has a man's pushbike frame wedged firmly in it. The frame stays upright thanks to the growth that has twisted and pushed its way through it. Each seems to support the other.

Sadly, amongst the stems and trunks of the hedge is the all too familiar sight of mankind's rubbish. Each hedge has its drinks bottles and drinks cans casually lying amongst the plastic bags and pages of old newspapers. That is very sad.

The plastic rubbish is bad enough, but I always feel that the glass bottles are top of the list when it comes to dangerous rubbish.

But these are field hedges; the garden hedges are neater, tidier, and less likely to be festooned with rubbish.

However, I have discovered, this doesn't apply to one or two of the hedges in some of my older gardens. Parking near them, I have noticed the odd pot or kettle nestling quietly amongst the branches.

They remind me so much of the hedge around my old granny's house.

These are not randomly thrown items, but artfully concealed and unusual homes for bird life. I have heard of birds nesting in these places and so it has been nice to see that some people are still supplying ready-made and recycled homes.

Strong Winds

The British are well known for being fascinated by the weather. If two of us meet up anywhere you can take it for granted the weather is mentioned in the first few sentences. It has come as no surprise therefore to find that several people I deliver to have decided to have little weather stations in their gardens.

Some are quite sophisticated, others less so. Most will tell you something about temperature, rainfall, and sunshine hours. The most common feature of them all though, is the anemometer.

One elderly chap I know got given a weather station for his birthday as an extra interest while he works in his garden.

'I leaves it over there,' he told me pointing at a flower bed in the middle of the lawn, 'The spinny thing that tells you what the wind speed is, helps keep the birds off the plants.'

He then proceeded to inform me that the station was no substitute for experience and for the 'twinges in me leg from a bit of shrapnel in Korea'.

For all that though, I know he used the station because he would often tell me how much sun we'd had or how much rain; he also told me how strong the wind had been.

The other day brought a sad turn of events.

'Well,' he told me as soon as I arrived, 'I reckon that wind last night must have got up to a hundred mile an hour, according to that weather station'.

I was impressed until he qualified the statement.

'I got out to check it this morning, only to find the spinny thing has vanished. It probably got across the Tamar before it hit the ground.'

I must say I have never laughed so much listening to weather reports on the telly or radio.

Summer Logs

I have been noticing amongst my customers the traditional summer activity of 'laying in' for the winter. Piles of logs are suddenly appearing in various gardens all around me. The thing is, these logs don't seem to have been bought; they're home grown.

As I delivered around the Roseland during that awful stormy weather of the beginning of the year, I witnessed a lot of rural devastation first-hand. Many of the properties I went to seemed to have bits of tree all over their gardens.

In a lot of cases, branches were the biggest problem. Many had broken completely away and fallen onto lawns and flower beds. Big, thick, and heavy, they crushed everything beneath them as they crashed down.

It is a sad sight to see these limbs torn away and no longer of use to the mother tree.

An even sadder sight were the places where a large tree had toppled completely in the wind. There is nothing elegant about falling down. When a person falls over, it always looks embarrassing, painful and a sudden shock. For the unfortunate person, it can leave confusion and misery in its wake... yet some people watching laugh.

With a tree it is much the same, except there is lasting sadness because there is no chance of repair – it is gone forever.

But we are a resourceful people. Once everything in the gardens and farms was tidied up and cleared away, the fallen branches and trees were left for a few months. They quietly dried out and awaited the sound of the chainsaw.

And now that time has arrived. It is almost as if everyone waited for the first person to start, because suddenly the air is rattling to the sound of many saws doing their work.

Out of the adversity of last winter has now come the fuel supply of this coming winter. I have loved watching this natural story unfold.

The Biggest Cat

Normally, I meet various animals when at work. They come in all sorts of different shapes and sizes, from horses and cattle down to a pet slug which was once brought out for me to coo over.

In a rural area such as ours, farm animals are as common as family pets. In the main however, it is the humble dog and cat that I come across the most.

Very early one morning I came across a young lady pulling at a lead. I stopped uneasily as she heaved at the lead and called the animal forward. Whatever the creature was, it had yet to come into view.

'It's not a dog,' she said, 'It's a cat.'

With that it stepped forward and came into view. It was a fully grown African lion, complete with mane. I froze.

'Don't be alarmed,' she smiled at me, 'He's very old and completely harmless; a family pet really. Let him sniff your hand.'

When you are only nineteen and you feel a lady needs to be impressed, what can you do?

I put my hand very gingerly in front of its nose and it sniffed my fingers. A tongue like wet sandpaper came out of its mouth and licked the back of my hand. He then lay down and half rolled onto his back.

'I told you he was a softy,' she laughed, 'He wants his tummy tickled.'

For the first and only time in my life, I crouched down and scratched a lion's belly and then tickled behind his ears.

'We let people pet him at the circus. He's a real favourite and kids love him.'

He may have been old and harmless, but it's not every day I pet an African lion in the British countryside.

The Boy

There is always a hierarchy in life and a group of old boys in the village I deliver to are no exception. All are retired, yet all keep busy. They spend their days pottering around in their own and other people's gardens, dispensing advice and criticism with equal measure.

I met them one morning while I was on delivery; they were digging over a vegetable plot.

'Where's number five?' I wondered as I walked in through the gate.

'Where's Bob gone? I hope you haven't buried him under that.' I pointed at the garden.

Billy raised himself up to his full height of five foot four and took his pipe out of his mouth before leaning on his fork. At 94 he is the oldest of the group working in the plot. This made him the spokesman.

The other three grinned and gurned at me as they too stood up from their digging. I'd never noticed before but each of them looked similar as they stood there. From top to toe they wore the same uniform and I had to hide a smile.

Wellington boots, corduroy trousers that started somewhere near their armpits, held up with belt and braces, tweed type jackets, shirt and tie, waistcoat, a cloth cap, and each had a pipe on the go. Each had either a spade or a fork in his hands; each looked as fresh as a daisy.

'Bob,' said Billy scratching his head, 'You mean the boy. The boy's making the tea, when it's coming up to break time and the men need a wet. The boy makes the tea.'

'I've made one for you too, son,' said a voice from the kitchen door as Bob walked through, balancing mugs, sugar bowl, and biscuits on a tray. Poor Bob; he'll always be the boy because he's only 89.

The Bull

A farmhouse I occasionally delivered mail to had a long driveway, fenced off between two fields that led up to the front door. Halfway up the drive were two openings opposite each other. This allowed the cattle to wander from field to field by crossing the drive, and two cattle grids kept them confined to that one bit of crossing.

I cycled back down the drive one morning from the house and found the bull standing between the two grids, meaning I couldn't get past. I stopped and we both stared at each other. He looked very threatening; I'm sure I looked very terrified.

I shouted 'Shoo,' loudly and he huffed through his nose, also very loudly. I then stamped my foot on the edge of the cattle grid and waved my arms at him. He stamped a hoof on the drive and waggled his ears at me. Pause.

Then I had a minor brainwave: I took off my jacket and waved it at him. I figured if they can do this in Spain then so can I. He must have seen the same film because he then lowered his head slightly.

I stared, he glared; I stepped forward onto the grid, he stepped forward and stopped just short of the grid; time passed as the impasse continued.

A noise of feet clattering behind me startled me and a four-year-old child, all gap-toothed and pigtailed, stomped passed me and confronted the bull.

'Billy... leave the pothtman alone,' she lisped as she slapped him on the shoulder area, 'He'th buthy and can't thtop and play.'

I don't know who was the most humiliated: the old bull who shuffled off into the field, head down; or the young, red-faced postman rescued by a lisping four-year-old.

The Dog Gang

There is a small pack of Springer spaniels on my duty. When I turn up at the farm they often appear in front of me for a 'good stare'. They are normally at least thirty yards away.

Those in the front row stare at me with belligerence in their eyes; a challenge if you like. They are the ones to beware of, if they should attack. They are the fighters.

But behind them and making sure they stay behind them, is the main threat.

This second group are the spear carriers; the loaders; the rabble rousers. They begin to bark and push against the front row as if encouraging them to 'have a go'. They are the ones who will start the attack only when the opponent is down.

I ignored them all for the first couple of days and just simply faced them and kept my eyes looking in their direction. The following day, I made my move.

Standing facing the pack I looked at them, then took two sharp paces forward. The response was instantaneous. With a movement that could only be described as panicky, the rear rank stopped barking, turned, and bolted across the yard to the safety of the barn.

The front rank paused for a moment and stared at me as I took another sharp step. Realising the back-up had now fled, and possibly wondering how they had been put in this position in the first place, they too turned and bolted.

I have never had any trouble from the dogs since and we seem to have become friends. There seems little difference between the pack of dogs in the yard and the occasional group of lads seen in a city centre. They all just need to know the boundaries.

The Eternal Circle

I find people very kind and charitable, especially those who live in small communities, such as villages. There just seems to be a greater sense that all who live there must pull together to help each other. This was how our village began to save plastic milk bottle tops.

As a village, we collected used stamps, postcards, clothing, even silver foil; there was always somebody who had an outlet for the stuff.

I don't remember when the word went out that there was a charity that was collecting the coloured plastic tops that identify the type of milk we drink. However, the village promptly started collecting them as well.

I would deliver mail to customers on refuse/recycling day and look through their recycling and take the bottle tops. How the collection of tops grew and grew.

The outlet for the bottle tops was our village pub. People would put any tops they had into a large bin containing a black bag. It soon got full. I asked the landlord where the tops went to. He told me that a customer of the pub took them to the school in the next village which were also collecting the things. He said they had an outlet for them.

He also pointed out that one chap he didn't know kindly brought in loads of the things.

Several months later I found myself delivering to the school in the other village. I commented on the amount of sacks containing bottle tops that the children were adding to.

'What outlet takes these then?' I asked.

'Oh,' she replied, 'We send them on to the pub in the village you live in. It's them that has the outlet.'

I sat back in my van and thought about it...then I laughed until I cried.

You couldn't make it up.

The Lonely Swan

Several days ago a flock of six or seven swans landed on the sea at St Mawes. They spent a good part of the day swimming happily, but by the following morning, all bar one of them had flown away.

I can only assume the one left had not heard the call to move on. She looked confused and sad as she swam a lonely wake around the harbour. Then she decided to climb out of the water and have a good look around. I don't think she was prepared for the consternation that she caused there.

People tried to lure her back into the sea by trails of food into the water. Did it work? Of course it did. The trouble was, she very quickly realised that she had found a food source.

A few days went by with her following a trail of crumbs into the sea, before getting out and heading back to the shops to continue the process.

Most seaside villages and towns have a seagull problem, with the cheeky birds swooping down on your pasty or your chips. It becomes more of a problem when it is a full-grown swan.

A week had gone by like this and the consensus was that she had lost her mate. She spent ages staring into windows and gazing at her reflection; then her attitude got a bit aggressive; and then she started to droop.

Thankfully someone realised she was sick and called the authorities in to check things out. Lead poisoning seems to be the judgement and she was taken away to be cured.

Mankind appears to have made her ill, and with the help of mankind, she will hopefully be made well. Once her treatment is finished she will be released. I really hope she makes it.

The Old Tarmac Road

Forty years ago, a council of the day authorised a new roundabout and road system near us. When all was finished, a 100-yard piece of road lay quietly abandoned off to one side of it. They even removed its cat's eyes.

Isolated by other roads into a large irregular island, the two fields either side of the old road lay largely unused. The old road was blocked off at both ends by a hedge, although one end had a gate set in to allow animal access.

Occasionally a small herd of cows or ponies would be brought by lorry and placed in the fields to graze. Only they and the odd walker ever put foot on that old bit of tarmac.

Fifteen years later I took a walk along it. No longer resembling a smooth main road, its tarmac lay fractured and cracked from the weather. Although it seemed to be crumbling gracefully away there was still a faint image of the white line remaining.

I last walked through that bit of ground about three years ago and nature is taking over the old road more and more. Crumbling from the outside in, potholed, and with grass and the odd sapling pushing its way through, it is well on its way to disappearing.

Nature seems to have a wonderful way of putting mankind firmly in its place. Whether it be by tsunami or earthquake; volcano or meteorite strike; or just a slow and gentle regression, nature has a way of letting us know that she is permanent and we are not.

It is a comfortable feeling to know that whatever we do, for ill or for good, nature will always be there to kind of tidy up afterwards.

Two Trout

Those who know me well are aware of just how squeamish I can be. I regret to say I am not a chap who can put an animal out of its misery. I can take a much-loved pet to the vet and let them do it; but I cannot do it myself.

When it comes to hunting, shooting or fishing, I'm useless.

I once heard a collie described as the great hunting dog with one flaw: it doesn't have the killing instinct. This is what makes it such a great herding animal.

I must be part collie because my killing instinct is notable by its absence.

It's inconsistent because I am not vegetarian and will eat meat in all its forms.

A few years ago a friend of mine and I met up at a pub for dinner and a chat. Mates since school, we like to catch up with each other every so often.

Gerry is a great countryman: he hunts, shoots and fishes, for the pot. We had been chatting for a while when we were asked what we would like for dinner.

We had both decided to order the trout. With no more ado, the waiter left and returned wheeling in a small fish tank and asked us to choose our fish.

Gerry pointed at two of them and they were deftly scooped out and placed into a smaller bowl to be taken away; then they both looked at me.

To this day he still tells people about the wide-eyed look on my ashen face as I stuttered that I would have the roast chicken instead. His last words are always, 'I'd love to have seen his face if they'd come to the table with an axe and a couple of chickens and asked him to choose which one.'

Wild Garlic

The advantage of having a rural job that keeps you on the move and in the great outdoors means that you have a constant variety of sights, sounds and smells to savour.

Couple this with visiting so many different properties in the course of a day and my life seems to be one long round of sensation and delight.

There is the astonishingly varied profusion of colour of so many flowers and leaves. Add to that, the background of white or pastel-painted cottages; or warm red brick houses; or dark-coloured stone walls.

So many gardens complement their houses; it's as if a painter had been at work as well as a gardener. Add a vivid blue sky or a blue sparkly sea as backdrop and perfection is on its way. These pictures take me right back to my boyhood.

Each and every day I hear birdsong all around me. The dawn chorus to the twilight call; each day is a musical delight. The cheerful sound of children playing, animals calling to each other, tractors in fields and lawnmowers in gardens, even the wind in the trees; all are reminders of carefree days from long ago.

There is no more nostalgic scent on a breeze than the smell of freshly-mown grass. Bringing back vivid memories, I find myself gazing back through the years wearing rose-tinted glasses. Were those days always as bright, warm, and sunny as my memory tells me?

The smell of pine is another memory-jerker. It evokes days of playing in the woods and I get reminded of the trees I climbed and fell out of as a boy.

So why do I have no memory at all of the deliciously wonderful smell of wild garlic that I smell today?

Unstoppable Meat

I was amused the other day to hear a description of a herd of cows that I had never imagined.

I was driving down a long private lane connecting several farms when I met one of the farmers walking towards me. We stopped and had a conversation.

'How long will you be before you come back up the lane to here again?'

'Only five minutes. No longer.'

'Try to make it in three, because when I open that gate you could find 'twenty tons of unstoppable meat' stampeding towards you.'

I shot off down the lane but couldn't help chuckling at his description of the herd. I have heard them referred to in all sorts of various ways, but twenty tons of unstoppable meat was a new one on me.

The more I thought of it the more I had to smile. I've seen enough cowboy films in my life to imagine and understand exactly what he meant.

I was a little fearful as I returned back up the lane. Visions of trying to explain away a crushed and hoof-battered van to an incredulous manager filled my thoughts as I drove along.

I got around yet another corner and saw the farmer trudging back down the lane towards me; alone.

We stopped and I spoke first this time.

'What happened to your twenty tons of unstoppable meat?'

'Stupid blasted creatures. They must have heard your van stop as you came down and thought it was me with food. As you drove off down the lane, they charged past me on the other side of the hedge and are now down at the other end of the field. They was unstoppable!!'

Not a frequently-used word in my dictionary, it got great usage that day.

Unwelcome Nesting

Every year there seems to be some report or other of birds nesting on the roofs, chimneys and ledges that make up people's homes. In the main it seems it is never a problem... unless the birds happen to be pigeons or seagulls. The mess engendered by both groups of birds, and the aggressive nature of the seagulls in particular when they have young about, invariably hits the headlines.

On many of the larger buildings I have noticed discreet netting protecting many of the alcoves and ledges. I have also spotted thin lengths of wire stretched across the roof lines where the birds might land and strut about.

On occasion, you can still see the forests of spikes laid out in rows that perform the same function.

All these devices, I think, are preferable to the cries of culling that comes in one suggested form or another.

On my rounds I have begun to notice these same protections on private houses now as well. The smaller songbirds and garden birds do not seem put off by these devices. On the contrary, they seem quite happy with the protection afforded by wire, spikes and netting.

It is amusing to see smaller birds flitting through the netting as a larger bird, or even hungry cat, has to stay outside.

No creature really needs to be destroyed when it proves itself a nuisance, especially if alternatives can be found. I have nothing against pigeons and seagulls; each have their own charms, although I am aware of the justification in the term 'sky rats'.

It is good though to see both groups of birds being encouraged to go away and thrive on the wilder areas of our landscape where they belong. 'Live and let live', I say.

White Cottages

As a youngster I always associated white cottages and houses with the seaside. I don't know why. On family visits and holidays to the more rural parts of the country, white painted cottages were everywhere: some with thatch; most tile or slate, but this was miles from the coast.

My Dad used to tell me that people painted cottages white to reflect away the sun. His view was that my great-granny's cottage would get stifling hot in a hot summer, and the reflective qualities of the white paint were what kept it cool.

I do remember as a child, after what seemed like hours running around the fields and woods, I would be scarlet with the heat. Yet when I staggered into her cottage, the coolness made goose bumps appear on my arms.

The cottage that Linda and I live in now is white painted and it looks lovely against the backdrop of green around our hedged village. It also remains very cool in the hot sunshine. I am not sure if this is the two-foot-thick walls or the white paint, but I will go with Dad's theory.

This idea of reflection of heat from the white walls was borne out the other day when I saw our local painter giving a row of white cottages a fresh coat.

The glare of the white paint in the sunshine hurt my eyes and made me squint; but this was as nothing to the poor painter. He stood manfully painting, eyes screwed up and with a small waterfall of perspiration pouring down his face.

His clothes were soaked with sweat and he was drinking water like a sponge.

'It's like I'm being BBQ'd', he whispered hoarsely.

I think my old Dad was probably right after all.

A Rescued Frog

I was getting ready to take my two young daughters to primary school one morning when they both hurtled into the kitchen demanding I save a frog from the family cat.

They dragged me outside, and there was our tomcat, tail lashing, and staring intently at a small green frog. Before he could pounce I managed to get over there and shoo the cat away.

Sadly, he only ran as far as the shed, before stopping and staring once more at the frog. Realising we couldn't leave the frog behind, I scooped it up into a bucket and threw a cloth over the rim top to keep it in. I promised both the girls that he could come with us and we would release him somewhere safe.

Five minutes later found me in the car and driving, as two concerned 'angels of mercy' sat in the back and watched the frog jumping up against the cloth.

Reassuring both of them that, 'No!! He can't escape so long as you leave the cloth over the bucket', we headed for a large pond that I knew.

We pulled up at the pond's edge but I was forbidden by two determined girls to let him go as a couple of swans were swimming slowly past. They convinced me that 'frog' is high on a swan's diet list.

Finally, we found a stretch of water near the road, devoid of other life, and we got out with the bucket. The girls held it over the water as I tugged the cloth off.

The frog leapt out and dived into the water.

His last sight had been of a lawn, flower bed, and angry cat. The look of astonishment on his face as he saw the water has stayed with me to this day.

A Hundred, Not Out

Not many of us reach the ripe old age of 100; and when you see how some behave you wonder how they made it.

She was a lovely lady, forgetful at times, and getting just a little tired and frail with the passage of time. I had been proud to deliver her card from the Queen on her last birthday.

Her daughter was in her late Seventies and the two of them lived together in the small cottage in the back of beyond.

Often I would spot the old lady asleep in her chair. I would walk quietly to the back door and put the post inside on the kitchen table without making a sound. Most days, if she was asleep it meant the daughter had popped down to the shops for something.

I got there once and was greeted by a sight that took my breath away. The daughter was obviously out because the old lady was walking determinedly towards me down the path on her own. Although she smiled at me I was almost afraid to move, as my eyes were drawn to the pair of garden shears she was carrying.

Obviously heavy, she had opened them and was resting both blades on her shoulders; one each side of her throat. She was clutching the handles.

'That withy sticking up out of the hedge is driving me mad. I thought I'd snip it off,' she smiled.

'Let me get it,' I interjected as I carefully lifted the shears from her throat, 'I can reach better.'

Moments later we walked arm in arm back to the house. I held the withy and the shears in my spare hand; she clutched her letters in hers.

The vision of those shears sitting on her shoulders haunts me still.

Three Noble Knights

It's not often you are called on to accept the challenge of three noble knights but it happened the other day. It was just after eight on a sunny Saturday morning when I pulled up at their house. I grabbed the mail, climbed out of the van, and headed up the path from their driveway to the front door.

Suddenly the door opened and the three knights paraded out onto the doorstep. Each wore a knight's helmet that partially obscured their face and each carried a wicked looking plastic sword. They stared in my direction and the middle one stepped forward brandishing a spare sword. He stopped and gazed at me before speaking.

'Do you want a sword fight against me and Amy and Molly?' he asked eagerly pointing his own sword in my direction and looking very fierce.

'Go on, Liam,' Amy grinned at me, 'Let's have a sword fight. We brought you a sword.'

'I'd love a sword fight,' I smiled at them, 'But not today. I can't do today. But one day next week I will, I promise; now, do you want to take the letters in for me?'

As befitting her six years of age Amy reached a hand out and took the letters. She gave one large letter to Thomas as he was next in age and only two years younger than her. Molly was given a little letter as it was felt that a three-year-old could probably only cope with that.

They all scampered into the house with the letters and I walked back to the van. I could never have had a swordfight that morning with the kids. I would have been arrested I'm sure. Each of them was wearing a knight's helmet, and a pair of sandals for the fight... and nothing else.

MERLIN UNWIN BOOKS

If you have enjoyed this book you might also like:

Fifty Bales of Hay Roger Evans

A View from the Tractor Roger Evans

A Farmer's Lot Roger Evans

A Job for all Seasons: my small country living Phyllida Barstow

My Animals and other Family: a rural childhood 1937-1956
   Phyllida Barstow

A Murmuration of Starlings Steve Palin

Living off the Land: country people 1850-1950
   Frances Mountford

Wild Flowers of Britain – month by month Margaret Wilson

Recollections of a Moorland Lad Richard Robinson

Beneath Safer Skies: a child evacuee in Shropshire Anthea Toft

WI Countrywoman's Year 1960 Elizabeth Paget

Land's End to John O'Groats Helen Shaw

The Flood: surviving the deluge Michael Brown

My Wood Stephen Dalton

Available from all good bookshops
Full details: **www.merlinunwin.co.uk**